IT WAS NEVER ABOUT BOOKS

Dolores,

I'm happy to call you my "old friend". God's blessings to you and your family.

Joy in Jesus!

IT WAS NEVER ABOUT BOOKS:
CONVERSATIONS BETWEEN A TEEN AND HER PASTOR

BY J. TAYLOR LUDWIG

AUSTIN, TEXAS

IT WAS NEVER ABOUT BOOKS:

CONVERSATIONS BETWEEN A TEEN AND HER PASTOR
BY J. TAYLOR LUDWIG

Cover and Interior Photographs:
Permission and thanks to Randal Solomon,
Studio7Network, St. Louis, Missouri
www.studio7network.com
Cover and Interior Model: Melissa Marie Gephardt
Cover graphics: Michael Qualben

Published by
LANGMARC PUBLISHING
P.O. 90488
Austin, Texas 78709-0488
www.langmarc.com

Library of Congress: 20059311258
ISBN: 1-880292971 $10.95

DEDICATION

This book is dedicated to all of
Pastor Rogahn's book tenders.
I hope you will share with others
what he shared with you—

the love of our Lord and Savior Jesus Christ.

CONTENTS

ACKNOWLEDGMENTS

I would like to thank my husband Rick for keeping the kids out of my hair for a few hours every evening for the six weeks it took to write this book.

I thank my brother Kevin Hayes for his contribution.

Thanks to Pastor Vernon Gundermann for reviewing a difficult chapter, and thanks to Pastor Rogahn's wife Su for reviewing the final manuscript.

Thank you to Randal Solomon of Studio7Network in St. Louis for gifting me with wonderful photos for this book.

Many thanks to Daniel Borkenhagen and Christopher Lieske for their invaluable help with research.

Thank you to Lois Qualben at LangMarc for her patience and kindness as I went through the publishing process for the first time.

And a very special thank you to Kathie Danker for a superb editing job, her encouragement, and for reminding me that this isn't my book, it's God's.

Most of all, I thank Pastor Rogahn for hiring a troubled book tender. I wish he could see what an impact he has made on my life.

A Teen's Journey

THE BOOK TENDER

It seems only fitting that I should be writing a book. I think of all the time I spent with him in his office tending to his books; now I'm writing one of my own about tending to his books, no less. I'm sure Pastor Rogahn would smile at the irony of it. But it's really not about the books. It's about what transpired as I tended to his books.

I was an eighth grader at Messiah Lutheran School in St. Louis in 1975, a troubled thirteen-year-old girl growing up in a dysfunctional family. Pastor Kenneth Rogahn instinctively sensed that I needed a positive male influence in my life when I sought work from him.

I needed two dollars for a field trip. I had asked my parents for the money, but they didn't have any. I told Pastor Rogahn about the field trip and asked if he had any chores I could do to earn some money. He told me that, as a matter of fact, the bookshelves in his office needed dusting, and he would pay me to dust them and clean the glass door panes.

It was quite a chore, as they were built-in bookshelves, eight doors across with sixteen panes of glass on each door. Pastor Rogahn sat at his desk and talked with me as we both worked on our own projects. He asked me a lot of questions about home and school, friends and family, and I gave him a lot of vague answers.

He did most of the talking, and I did most of the listening. I finished as quickly as I could, collected my two dollars, and left.

About a week later, after a Wednesday morning chapel service, Pastor Rogahn asked me to stop by his office after school. When I arrived, he told me he needed me to tend to his books. He wanted the hardbacks separated from the paperbacks and would pay me a dollar to do the job. He said he thought his bookshelves would look much nicer arranged that way, but he didn't have the time to make the change himself. There didn't appear to be that many paperbacks. How hard could it be? I took the job, and again we had an interesting discussion as we both worked.

A couple of weeks later, I was summoned to Pastor Rogahn's office again to tend to his books. He thought his bookshelves would look better if the books were arranged by size, from smallest to largest. So we both got to work at our tasks, and we talked.

He called me to tend to his books again. They didn't look right to him for some reason. He wanted me to rearrange them from largest to smallest. Then I was called in a couple weeks later to dust his bookshelves and clean the glass door panes again. I was now tending to his books about every two to three weeks.

Pastor Rogahn decided he didn't care for the size arrangement and wanted the books arranged by colors. After many color-arranging sessions, he finally seemed pleased with a pattern in which all his red books came first. Then it was time to dust the bookshelves again and clean the glass door panes. There was always something that needed to be tended to with his bookshelves or his books, and always we talked.

I started high school. One day I walked into his office to find a large box of index cards sitting on the table. He wanted them placed in all of his books to serve as bookmarks. We chatted as I placed the index cards, and he sat at his desk and worked.

I continued to tend to the pastor's books during my sophomore year, although less often because I was involved in a few extracurricular activities. With the bookmarks, he found all kinds of things he needed done to his books. He needed the title of the book written on each bookmark in case it should get misplaced. Then he thought it would also be nice to add the author's name to the bookmarks. Later I added the number of pages in each book and a host of other useless information. And always the bookshelves needed to be kept dusted and the glass door panes cleaned. And always we talked and talked and talked.

It had taken Pastor Rogahn nearly the whole first year of my tending to his books for him to get me to really open up to him, but over the next couple of years I started to share more and more with him.

I had tended to his books for nearly three years when I landed a job at a local theater. I didn't know how I was going to break the news to him. I knew how important his books were to him, and he had told me I was the best book tender a pastor could ever hope to find. Also, I couldn't stand the thought of someone else replacing me. I approached him cautiously, looking at the floor as I talked. I said, "I'm sorry, Pastor, but I got a real job, so I guess I won't be able to tend to your books anymore."

He smiled, hugged me, pulled me back at arm's length, and said, "I'll tell you what, Judi, why don't you call me if you ever need to tend to my books."

It took a minute for his words to sink in. So *that* was what all this book tending had been about! He had been doing it for my benefit, not his. He had been serving as my mentor for three years, and he had paid me to be on the receiving end of his caring spirit. I said something to him about lying to me, and he assured me that he would never lie to me for any reason, even to avoid hurting my feelings. He said, "I really did enjoy watching my bookshelves being transformed." I think he really liked watching me being transformed, and so did I.

Over the years I did call Pastor Rogahn to seek his counsel and advice, to make confessions, to share triumphs and trials, and each time I would request the appointment with the excuse, "Pastor, I need to tend to your books." The pretense of tending to the books was over, but it was still my habit to hang around the bookshelves as I talked with him, even opening the glass panel doors and running my hands across the books as we talked. If I had a confession to make and couldn't look him directly in the eye, I would sit on the floor next to the bookshelves and arrange the books in various ways as we talked.

I recently visited Pastor Rogahn's former office at Messiah. The furniture has changed, but the bookshelves are just as I remember them. I remarked to the secretary that the office lacked the warmth that I remember from the days when Pastor Rogahn was there. She replied, "It isn't the room that gave the office its warmth. It was the spirit of the people inside the room."

I suppose she's right. When Pastor Rogahn was in that room, I always felt safe and warm. He was a wonderful man who had some great insights into some of life's toughest questions. He answered many of them for me as I tended to his books, and I would like to pass his insights on to you.

EIGHTH GRADE

FRIENDS

Pastor Rogahn was sitting at his desk, leafing through the mail. "Hi, old friend," he said as he smiled and greeted me as he had nearly every time I entered his office. "How are you today?"

"Why do you call me your old friend?" I asked, laying my books and jacket on the table and walking over to stand by his desk. It was obvious I wasn't old; I was just thirteen. And we certainly weren't old friends as if we went way back.

"Every friend is a new friend who will someday *be* an old friend," he said, pulling out a trash can from underneath his desk and tossing in a flyer.

"And we're not really friends, you know. You're my parents' age, so we *can't* be friends," I told him. "It's not like we hang out together or anything."

"We can't be friends?" He dropped the mail he was holding, held his hands across his heart and pouted as if I had hurt him deeply. "Why do you say that?"

"Because you're old." He was forty-two, my age as I write this, although he looked a bit older because he was nearly bald.

"I can't be friends with you just like I can't be friends with a six year old," I reasoned. "It's not like we can do stuff together."

I picked up a letter that had fallen on the floor and placed it back on his desk. I figured I had set him straight, so I walked over to the table by the bookshelves, pulled out a chair, and sat down. He hadn't given me my book-tending assignment yet, and I was in no hurry to get started. I picked up a magazine from the table and started looking through it while I waited for him to tell me what he wanted me to do with his books.

He thought about my statement for all of about one minute. "Maybe you can't be friends *with* a six-year-old child," he said. "It wouldn't be an age-appropriate relationship for you, Judi. You're not interested in the same things as a six year old. But you could be a friend *to* a six year old. If her ball went into the street, you could be a friend *to* her and go and retrieve it. So perhaps since our relationship is not an age-appropriate one either, we could be friends *to* each other."

"Okay, so if your ball goes into the street, I'll go and retrieve it," I said.

"You get the picture." He walked over to the table, pulled out a chair across from me, and sat down. He leaned back and crossed his legs. "But I'm not your only friend, Judi. Jesus is your friend, too," he said.

"I've got lots of friends!" I snapped back.

The truth was I didn't have any real friends. I didn't fit into either gender group. I hung out with the boys, but they would let me participate in their games only if they needed an extra player. Most of the time I sat on the sidelines and watched. When I hung around the girls, I felt uncomfortable. I didn't know what to talk about. They used me as a go-between with boys they liked but were afraid to talk to. Adults called me a tomboy. Some of the boys called me "Butch." Only my long, blond hair indicated that I might be a girl. I was confused at times as to whether I was a boy or a girl. I prayed for God to make me a boy.

"Of course you have friends," he said, "but hopefully not so many that you can't add me to your list—and Jesus, too."

"Great, I'll add to my list two more friends who I can't hang out with."

If he caught my sarcasm, his face didn't show it. "I promise I'll be a friend to you, Judi, and Jesus will be a friend to you, too."

"I guess He'll go retrieve my ball from the street."

Pastor Rogahn didn't laugh at my old joke. He uncrossed his legs and leaned forward in the chair, resting his forearms on the table and folding his hands as he looked me directly in the eye.

"When all of your other friends have deserted you, when they're nowhere to be found, Jesus will still be there for you. When you need someone to talk to, He will listen. When you have a secret that you don't think you can trust with anyone else, you can trust Him with it. When you don't think anyone could possibly understand whatever it is you're going through at home or at school, Jesus will understand. Jesus will be your friend."

I had never really thought about Jesus as being my friend before. I knew He was God's Son and had died for my sins and that if I believed in Him, I would go to heaven. We always sang that song in church, "What A Friend We Have In Jesus," but it was just a song.

"We sometimes sing 'What A Friend We Have In Jesus' in church," I said.

"Yes, we do, and we could just as easily sing 'What a Friend We Have In Pastor Rogahn.' He stood to return to his desk, pleased that I was at least willing to add Jesus to my list of friends, if not him.

I laughed at his joke, which seemed really funny to me at the time but sounds corny to me as I'm writing this. He seemed to share my dry sense of humor.

"But, Pastor, if me and Jesus are going to be friends to each other, how am I going to be a friend to Him?" I thought I could stump him with that one. "It's not like He's going to share His problems and secrets with me."

"That's easy," he replied, as he sat back down at his desk. "You can be a friend to Jesus by telling others about Him so that He can become their friend, too."

"And should I tell others about you, too, about what a friend they have in Pastor Rogahn?"

He put his hand up to his mouth in a mock whisper. "Let's not let the word get out that I'm a nice guy."

He dropped his hand and looked at me in all seriousness. "So, Judi, are you saying we can be friends?"

"I guess so." I laid my magazine down and stood up to get to work. "Maybe we can't be friends *with* each other, but we can be friends *to* each other," I said, giving him a dose of his own words. "We can retrieve each other's balls and stuff. I've never been a friend to a pastor before. You're my first pastor friend. I guess I can be a friend to you today by tending to your books. What do you want me to do?"

"I'm honored to call you my friend," Pastor Rogahn said, and then added, "my *old* friend. And I think my bookshelves would look nice if I had all my green books arranged on the upper shelves. What do you think?"

He didn't have too many green books. He had a four-volume set of *Christian Dogmatics*, which might take up one shelf, but there probably weren't even enough green books to cover the whole top row. It was going to be an easy job.

"I think the green books are the way to go, Pastor. You'll probably set a trend for all the other pastors out there."

He smiled. It was a smile I was to see a lot over the next twelve years as he became my best friend. I was never *his* best friend. I guess he had his wife for that—and Jesus. But he was my best friend. The qualities he told me that Jesus possessed as a friend were the very qualities that Pastor Rogahn possessed. When I needed someone to talk to, he would listen. I could trust him with my secrets. The things I thought no one else would possibly understand, he understood. We never hung out together. We never did stuff together. But it didn't matter. He was a friend to me. He was my old friend, Pastor Rogahn.

BOOKS

Books, books, and more books. Pastor Rogahn sure had a lot of books, and they weren't all theology either, although the majority were. He had books on a variety of subjects and even a few novels.

"Pastor, why do you have so many books?" I asked him one day while I was arranging his books according to their size. That day he wanted them arranged from largest to smallest on a shelf by shelf basis, which was a lot easier than some of the other arrangements I had done for him.

"They're not all mine," he replied. "Some belong to the church. Others I kept from college and my years at the seminary. Some were given to me as gifts, and some I bought for myself."

"But why do you keep all of them? You aren't going to read them all again, are you?" I inquired, as I removed a few books and laid them on the table so I had some working room on one of the shelves.

"I keep them so you can arrange them nicely for me on my shelves," he said. He smiled as he twirled a pen around in his hands. "Actually, some of them I refer to quite often. Others I keep because they're part of a collection. Others because they were gifts. There are lots of reasons."

"What's your favorite book?" I asked.

"The Bible," he replied.

"I should've known you'd say that," I said, with a smirk of disbelief. "But you're just saying that because you're a pastor. Tell me what your favorite book really is."

"The Bible," he answered again, without cracking a smile.

"You say it's your favorite book, Pastor, but I bet you haven't even read it all the way through. I don't know anybody who has read the whole Bible, not even a pastor."

He did have no fewer than ten Bibles on his bookshelves. They used to be all in one place, but now that I was tending to his books he would have to remember where to find them by their size, color, or whatever other distinguishing characteristic by which I had arranged them.

"They made me read the whole thing at the seminary," he said. "It was a requirement for my major." His attempt at humor flew over my head. "But I had read it before then, I've read it since then, and I'm still reading it. And you're still reading it, aren't you? Don't you read from the Bible at school?"

"We do," I said, as I began rearranging another shelf. "But it's not my favorite book."

"What is your favorite book, Judi?" He stopped playing with the pen and looked at me as if he genuinely wanted to know.

"*The Adventures of Huckleberry Finn,*" I replied. "It's by a guy named Mark Twain. He's from Missouri, like me."

"*Huckleberry Finn* is one of my favorite books, too," Pastor Rogahn said. "Tell me what you liked about the book."

"Everything," I said, pleased that Pastor Rogahn liked my favorite book and surprised that he read adventure stories.

"It's just a really neat adventure story, and I thought it was pretty funny, too. Remember when Huck dressed up like a girl? That was pretty funny. And those guys Duke and Dauphin and when Huck and Tom were trying to free Jim, but he was already free. . ."

I was laughing out loud remembering my favorite parts of *Huckleberry Finn*. Pastor Rogahn was smiling.

"How many times have you read *Huckleberry Finn*, Judi?" he asked me as he tapped his ink pen on the desk.

"Three times," I said, holding up three fingers. "I've read *Tom Sawyer*, too, but I think *Huckleberry Finn* is a lot funnier. I liked it better."

"Me, too," Pastor Rogahn agreed. "And I'll bet the second time you read *Huck Finn*, you caught some details you missed the first time you read it. And I would bet the third time you read it, you learned even more."

"I don't know, maybe."

"Sure you did." He stopped tapping his pen and pointed it at me. "Okay," he said, "the widow Huck lives with at the beginning of the story, I don't recall her name offhand, although I'm sure you do. But do you remember the name of her sister?"

"That's easy," I answered, "Miss Watson, and the widow is the Widow Douglas."

"You see, you know that because you've read the book three times. You remember more details every time you read it. You liked the book the first time you read it, but you still enjoy reading it even though you know everything that's going to happen because you always pick up details with each reading that you missed on the previous reading. That principle could be applied to any book. No matter how many times you've read it, you can still learn something new from it.

"The first time I read *Huckleberry Finn* I was about your age, Judi, and I thought it was a great adventure story. When I read it again in high school, I thought it was a nice reflection on friendship. When I read it in college, I thought it was making a statement about race and morality. When I read it as an adult, I thought Twain had captured society's hypocritical principles.

"You've given me the desire to read the book again, and I bet I'll learn something new once more. That's how it is with my favorite book, the Bible."

He walked over to the bookshelves and picked up a medium size, black Bible from one of the lower shelves, took it back to his desk, and started browsing through it.

"The Bible is a different book every time I read it. I always learn something new. And talk about adventure! My favorite book is packed full of travels and adventures, not to mention stories of friendships, celebrations, wars, and romances. You name it, and God's book has it," he said, patting his favorite book.

"I like some of the stories from the Old Testament," I said, "like about Noah's ark and Daniel in the lion's den, but some of that stuff about Moses and all those people wandering around in the wilderness is pretty boring."

"Boring? We must not be talking about the same book," Pastor Rogahn said. "I'm talking about the Bible. There are a lot of books written by men. But this is the only book, think about it, the *only* book, on this whole planet in which every word was inspired by God. Paul writes in II Timothy that, 'All Scripture is given by inspiration of God.' I believe many Christian books are inspired by God, but the Bible is the only book in which every single word has been breathed by God.

"That's why I want to read it again, and again, and again. I want to read it and think about it and digest every single word God has to say to me, and then read it and think about it and digest it again. We're talking about God here. We're talking about our Creator. We're talking about the Father of Jesus. And we're talking about His book."

The pastor had as much passion for the Bible as I had for *Huckleberry Finn*. I decided it was inconsiderate of me to call his favorite book boring. He hadn't criticized my favorite book. I decided I had hurt his feelings, and I would try to patch things up.

"You know, Pastor, it's probably going to take me my entire life to read the whole Bible," I said, "but since you're going to read my favorite book again, I guess I could read one of your favorite Bible stories. I really like adventure stories. Maybe you can think of an adventure story from the Bible that I might like."

"I can," he said, without hesitation. "I suggest you read the book of Mark. It's a wonderful adventure story I know you'll enjoy. It tells of the adventures of a man named Jesus."

"Give me a break, Pastor. I already know the story of Jesus," I whined. "There's got to be some adventure story in that Bible I haven't read yet. Besides, I never agreed to read a whole book from the Bible. I just said I'd read one of the stories."

"A story is different every time you read it, Judi, just like *Huckleberry Finn*. I'll bet you pick up details reading about Jesus this time that you missed the last time you read about Him, and I can almost guarantee you'll learn something new. I'll read *Huckleberry Finn* again, and we can discuss our favorite adventure stories some more."

I went back to work organizing the pastor's books while he sat at his desk, reading his favorite book. I only had one section left to finish, but my heart just wasn't in it. Even though I had volunteered to read one of the pastor's favorite stories, I couldn't help but feel like I'd been had. I felt as though I had just been given a homework assignment, and it wasn't as if I didn't have enough homework to do already.

I kept my word and read the book of Mark, and Pastor Rogahn read *Huckleberry Finn* again. I actually finished his book before he finished mine, and we talked about our favorite stories over several book-tending sessions.

My favorite book has changed over the years as I have matured. *Huckleberry Finn* is still one of my all-time favorites, but today the Bible is also at the top of my list.

As for Pastor Rogahn, he was never as fickle as I. He remained a devoted fan of the Bible, which he still insisted was his favorite book years later. When I'd tell him about a good book I'd read, he'd always say, "I'm in the middle of a good book, too. It's a great adventure story. Perhaps you'd like to read it."

"I've read it, Pastor. I've read it again and again. And you're right. I learn something new every time I read it. I pick up more details about Jesus that I missed the last time I read about Him, and the Bible is a different book every time I read it."

FORGIVENESS

I wasn't arranging the pastor's books today. I was leafing through for notes and scraps of paper he'd left in them during his readings and research. I was surprised at how much I was finding. He didn't want anything thrown away. He had given me a box to put everything in and had retired to his desk.

"Are you and Mr. Taylor getting along any better?" he asked as soon as he sat down.

Bryant Taylor was the fifth- and sixth-grade teacher at Messiah. I had recently been suspended for throwing a firecracker at him. I had just wanted to scare him, but the firecracker had burned a hole in the shirt he was wearing. He had called my parents, and they had paid for the shirt.

"I hate him," I said. "He lied about how much that shirt cost. Nobody pays fifteen dollars for a shirt. He's just a big cry baby. I'm never gonna forgive him for calling my parents." I took a stack of books to the table to sort through as we talked.

"First of all, Judi, you don't hate him. Hate is a very strong word. Maybe you dislike him. And Mr. Taylor is a Christian. He didn't lie about how much his shirt cost.

You told me he bought it at Famous Barr. That's what a nice dress shirt would cost there. Now let's talk about who needs to forgive whom."

"I'll never forgive him. I'll hate him as long as I live, Pastor. He's not even my teacher, so he had no right to call my parents. He could've told Mr. Bremer, and he could've called them. At least they're used to getting calls from him. Anyway, there's no law that says I have to forgive him. It's not like I'll go to jail or anything." I found an old receipt in one of the books and tossed it into the box.

"Maybe you won't go to jail, Judi, but you could go to hell. Mr. Taylor has forgiven you for throwing the firecracker at him. Now you need to forgive him for calling your parents. What do we say when we pray the Lord's Prayer? Forgive us as we forgive others. Jesus said if you don't forgive others, then God won't forgive you. If you don't forgive Mr. Taylor, then you are cutting yourself off from God's forgiveness."

"It's hard to forgive someone you don't like, Pastor, and I just don't like the guy."

"I never would have guessed. But it's dangerous to hold a grudge because God forgives us in the same measure as we use to forgive others. Jesus never held a grudge. Did you know that the very first words Jesus spoke from the cross were, 'Father, forgive them, for they do not know what they are doing'? While being crucified, he pleaded with God to forgive those who were responsible for His being there.

"You *can* forgive Mr. Taylor because the Holy Spirit will help you. He will make you willing and able to forgive. Say, 'I forgive you, Mr. Taylor.'"

"I forgive you, Mr. Taylor," I mumbled.

"Was that so hard?"

"But I don't really mean it."

"Trust God to make it happen. If you repeat it over and over again in your head twenty, thirty, forty times a day, you'll find that by the end of the week you will mean it. God will remove the bitterness from your heart. Give it a try."

"Okay, Pastor."

I did try it, and not only was I able to forgive Mr. Taylor for something I never should have been upset about in the first place, but I actually started to like him. He had every right in the world to call my parents. When I forgave him and began to treat him with more respect (no more firecracker throwing), he was kinder to me. He was a talented young athlete who taught me a powerful over-handed volleyball serve that led our small Lutheran girls' team to the championship finals.

Thanks, Mr. Taylor.

COMMUNION

Pastor Rogahn was filling out a form. "I'll be with you in a moment, Judi. Let me finish what I'm doing here."

I walked around to the other side of his desk to look at the pictures on the wall. There was an old one of Messiah Church taken from the sky when the church had first been built. There was another of Jesus on his knees, praying with three of His disciples. But it was the painting of "The Last Supper" that I really liked. I had seen it before, but this was the first time I had ever really studied it.

Pastor Rogahn completed his form and asked if I was ready to start working. I wasn't. I had questions about the painting.

"Pastor, why did Jesus and all His disciples eat on the same side of the table? They look like they're all crowded together. How come half of them didn't eat on the other side, across from Him?"

Pastor Rogahn walked over and stood beside me. He studied the painting, which he'd probably seen hundreds of times before.

"I would guess da Vinci wanted to show all of their faces. If half the disciples were sitting across from Jesus, we'd be looking at their backs."

He stared at the painting for a long time. "Let's go into the church, Judi. I'd like to show you something."

I followed him into the sanctuary and up the first few steps to the altar. Sculpted across the front of the marble altar was "The Last Supper." I don't know why I had never noticed it before. It was fairly large. I guess when I took communion, I usually gazed at the crucifix above the altar. Pastor Rogahn closed the middle communion gates and suggested we kneel at the rail. We knelt in the center, directly across from the sculpture of Jesus.

"Okay, Judi," Pastor Rogahn said, "who's across the table from Jesus now?"

"We are," I answered.

"Yes, we are. Isn't it wonderful? Every time we come to the Lord's table for Holy Communion, we eat and drink the Lord's Supper with Him. He has left a place on the other side of the table for us to join in the feast. All we have to do is accept the invitation to join Him. Now, why don't you join me in prayer?"

We folded our hands, bowed our heads, and Pastor Rogahn prayed, "Father, thank You for inviting us to Your table. Please lead us to accept Your invitation every time it is extended, to receive the body and blood of Your Son Jesus Christ for the forgiveness of all our sins. In Jesus' Name we pray. Amen."

Messiah once had two benedictions during its services, one before and one after Holy Communion for those who did not wish to commune. Pastor Rogahn announced that he felt uncomfortable saying a benediction *before* Holy Communion because the service was not over. He said he would have a moment of silence for those who wished to leave, but they would not leave with God's blessing until after the Lord's Supper had been served.

I was one who would, occasionally after a long service, leave after the first benediction. Since kneeling with Pastor Rogahn at the communion railing, I have seldom declined an invitation to the feast.

GUILT

I was having trouble concentrating on my book-tending assignment. It was a tough one. I was to arrange the books in alphabetical order by title, and this was the second session I had been working on it. This arrangement sounded like the most logical one to me. It would make any book easy to find. But I secretly hoped Pastor Rogahn wouldn't be satisfied with it, because I was really starting to enjoy tending to his books, and I could use the dollar.

Something had really been bothering me. I had wanted to ask him about it, but I didn't know how. I decided to turn it into a hypothetical question. Yeah, that was the way to do it, hypothetically. I waited for a moment when he was just shuffling papers around on his desk, looking like he needed something to keep him occupied.

"Pastor, I've got a hypothetical question for you," I said, my words coming out as fast as I could say them. "If somebody cheated on a test, let's say a spelling test just to give an example, and they confessed it to God and said they were sorry and He forgave them, but then they went and did it again and confessed it again and said they were sorry, would He forgive them again? Or would He think they weren't really sorry because they did it again? And then, if they weren't forgiven, and they were walking home from school and were hit by a bus and killed, would they go to hell because they weren't forgiven? Or, if they lived, could they do something good to make up for it?"

There, I had gotten the whole hypothetical thing out. He stopped shuffling his papers and just held them with both hands. He looked at me for what seemed like an eternity before he spoke.

"I'd assume they were truly repentant if they said they were sorry," Pastor Rogahn said, speaking very slowly, clearly thinking about each word before he said it, "and that God would forgive them. But being repentant means they are sorry they committed that sin, and they don't intend to commit it again. We can be forgiven for committing the same sin a second, third, or however many times as long as we are truly sorry for our sins.

"Why don't you put down those books, grab a chair, and come sit with me for a minute," he said.

I did as he asked and brought a chair around to the side of his desk. He put his papers down and turned around to face me.

"Judi," he said, "Salvation is so simple most people don't get it. It's not based on anything *we* do. It's based on what Jesus did for us.

"It's obvious to me from your hypothetical question that something's bothering you. Would you like to discuss it?" he asked.

"Not really," I said. "I think you pretty much answered it. Thanks."

And he had answered it. I was pretty sure that if I got killed by a bus on the way home, I wouldn't go to hell because Jesus had died for my sins. I was halfway out of the chair when Pastor Rogahn gently touched my arm and held it for a second. I fell back in the chair.

"You don't have to discuss anything with me you don't want to," he said. "But something closely related to your hypothetical question is guilt. And it's okay to feel guilty about something. It means our conscience is in good working order. But if we do something long enough, or if we do something enough times, we'll stop feeling guilty about it. It doesn't matter what sin it is we're talking about. In your hypothetical question, you used a spelling test as an example. Let's stick with that. If we cheat on enough spelling tests enough times, we'll stop feeling guilty about cheating. Do you understand what I'm trying to tell you, Judi?"

"No," I admitted. I didn't have a clue.

"Let me put it a different way," he said. "Guilt isn't entirely a bad thing, because it leads us to want to confess and repent of our sins to God. But once we're forgiven we need to let go of the burden of guilt. It's a monkey on our back. We're guilty of sin, but Jesus bore our guilt on the cross. We can let go of the guilt now. We're forgiven. I'm forgiven, and you're forgiven. Say it, 'I'm forgiven.'"

"I'm forgiven," I repeated.

"And you are, you know. I forgive you, and God forgives you. Now let's get back to work and turn all this hypothetical nonsense over to Jesus. We've got books to tend to. Are you even up to the G's yet?"

I was all the way up to the L's. *Law and Gospel, The Life and Epistle of St. Paul, The Life and Times of Jesus,* and then I could fill the shelves with fifty-four volumes of *Luther's Works.* It went a lot faster with that darn monkey off my back.

NONCONFORMISTS

"I think you're probably the first true nonconformist I've ever met," Pastor Rogahn said to me as I tended books for him one afternoon in early June. I was a month shy of my fourteenth birthday.

He had greeted me in his customary manner and had given me my book-tending assignment. He wanted his books arranged with the blue ones first. Then he had settled in at his desk to work. About fifteen minutes had passed without a word between us.

"Now, I've met lots of people who have claimed to be nonconformists," he continued, without looking up at me from whatever it was he was working on, "but they've always ended up going along with the group in some fashion or another. But I haven't seen that with you."

"What's a nonconformist?" I asked, setting a pile of books down on the table while I waited for his reply.

"It's a person who doesn't always follow the rules or customs of a society or group," he answered, impressing me with his ability to write while he was carrying on a conversation with me.

"I obey most of the rules at school," I protested. "Once in awhile Mr. Bremer will catch me chewing gum or talking, but that's about it."

I cleared some more books off the shelves and piled them on the table so I could start his blue arrangement with *Matthew Henry's Commentary*. It was a six-volume set and would take up most of the first shelf.

"That's not what I mean," Pastor Rogahn said. He was now leaning back in his chair with his hands clasped behind his head. "Take confirmation, for example. All the other girls wore dresses, but you wore pants. And I'm not saying there's anything wrong with that; I'm just saying it might lead one to believe you're a nonconformist."

He was right. I had told my parents I wouldn't be confirmed if I had to wear a dress. My mother had called Pastor Rogahn, and he had said I could wear slacks. Girls weren't allowed to wear pants during a confirmation ceremony back then, so I realize as I'm writing this that Pastor Rogahn had to have been a nonconformist himself to have allowed me to wear the slacks. On the other hand, he told me I would not be allowed to attend the reception following the service. I guess he had reasoned not too many members would see me out of my robe if I left right away.

"Forgive me if I hurt your feelings, Judi. Being a nonconformist isn't necessarily a bad thing. There are some people right here at Messiah who might say that I am a nonconformist."

"You?" I asked, hardly able to believe a pastor would break society's rules. "No way." I set a big stack of *Luther's Works* on the table and sat down to take a break. I wanted to hear this.

"Were you in church on Easter Sunday?"

"Yes."

"Did you enjoy the sermon?"

"Yes," I replied, honestly. I wasn't trying to stroke his ego. I really had enjoyed the sermon. It was different, that was for sure. When it was time for Pastor Rogahn to appear in the pulpit to give his sermon, he was nowhere to be found. After a considerable amount of time had gone by, Pastor Rogahn said, "Hey, I'm back here everybody. I'm back in the narthex. Boy, I wonder how the people felt when they found the tombstone rolled back, and Jesus wasn't where *He* was supposed to be."

I don't remember any of the sermon after that because I just sat there thinking how the people must have felt. I could *feel* how they must have felt when Jesus wasn't in that tomb. It was the same feeling I got wondering where Pastor Rogahn was all that time he was supposed to be in the pulpit.

"That was a great sermon, Pastor. I mean it. It was really good."

"Thank you. I thought so," he said, without a trace of arrogance, as he got up and walked over to the filing cabinet. I started removing the rest of the red volumes of *Luther's Works* from the shelves.

"But there are those who didn't. Because it wasn't a traditional sermon a pastor would give, some people might say I'm a nonconformist, just as they might say you're a nonconformist because you wear jeans to church on Sundays."

"Well if you're a nonconformist, then I guess it's not bad to be one," I said.

"You misunderstood me, Judi. I never said I was a nonconformist. I said people might infer that I am by some of my actions. I prefer to think of myself as creative," he smiled at me as he pulled a folder from the filing cabinet and sat back down at his desk.

"I don't want to be a nonconformist either," I said. "I think I'm creative, too."

It sounded to me as though he were telling me that people thought I was a nonconformist and I *was*, and that people thought he was a nonconformist and he *wasn't*. I wasn't sure I liked that.

"Life isn't always easy for the nonconformist," Pastor Rogahn said. "It's always easier to go along with the group. Jesus was a nonconformist, you know."

"No way!" I argued. "Jesus always obeyed all the rules. He never sinned."

"He always obeyed His Father's rules, and no, He never sinned, but He didn't always conform to society's rules," Pastor Rogahn said. "He was a nonconformist as far as man's laws were concerned. For example, He healed people on the Sabbath when it was against the law to work on the Sabbath. And look at some of the tax collectors and people with whom He associated. Preachers during Jesus' time didn't gather with people they alleged to be sinners, even though we are all sinners, of course. So He wasn't conforming to others' perceptions of a preacher."

I had all but forgotten about tending to the books. I was too wrapped up in our discussion, and Pastor Rogahn hadn't yet opened the file folder on his desk.

"Jesus paid for being a nonconformist, Judi. He was beaten and whipped and nailed to a cross. Most people are conformists, so they don't know what to do with the nonconformist. Anytime someone is perceived to be different in any way, people feel that person is a threat to the safety and security of their group."

"Jesus could've gotten down from that cross anytime He wanted to," I reminded him.

"Yes, He could have, but He was conforming to His Father's wishes to save us from our sins and grant us eternal life. Jesus wasn't a nonconformist all the time. Not too many people are. Life would be pretty difficult for the person who never tried to fit in with the group and wanted to be a nonconformist all the time. I sure wouldn't want to be, and I wouldn't think you would, either."

I didn't answer him. I wanted to ask him to give me some more examples of how Jesus was a nonconformist, but he had opened the file folder and had begun writing, so I knew our discussion had ended.

But I learned a new word, "nonconformist," and had been compared to both Pastor Rogahn and Jesus, the highest praise I could ask for. But there was one more question that was begging to be asked.

"Pastor, does arranging your books with all the blue books first make you a nonconformist?"

He started laughing. "No," he said. "Now, if I arranged my books with all of my red books first, then I would be a nonconformist."

SINNERS

Pastor Rogahn wanted his books in a rainbow arrangement. I didn't have to stick with a particular pattern, although I was trying to as long as I had enough colors. It was actually fairly easy, and I was having fun with it.

The pastor had several books stacked on his desk. One was lying open, and he kept glancing at it as he wrote notes on a memo pad. He was wearing his clerical collar today, and he looked like a pastor to me, almost saintly. I stared at him for a long time. Finally he looked over at me.

"Is there a problem, Judi?"

"No, Pastor, I was just wondering. . . do you ever sin?"

"Of course not. I'm perfect."

He started writing again, and then he began laughing.

"Yes, I sin. Pastors are sinners, too, just like everyone else."

"I can't picture it, Pastor. I just can't see you doing anything bad," I said. "When's the last time you sinned?"

"Today," he replied.

"While you were dressed in your pastor uniform?!"

"Judi," he chuckled, "we all sin daily in thought, word, or deed. I'm no different from you or anyone else."

"Have you ever broken one of the Ten Commandments?" I asked.

"Yes."

"Which one?"

"All of them," he answered.

"Pastor! You murdered somebody!"

"No, Judi, I didn't kill anyone. But when we break one of God's commandments, we're guilty of breaking all of His commandments."

"I just can't believe you're a sinner, Pastor. You sure don't look like one. You could've fooled me."

"Maybe I could have fooled you, but I can't fool God. He knows I'm a sinner. He knows we're all sinners. That's why he sent His Son to die for us. God offers us grace and forgiveness for our sins through Jesus."

"I know all that stuff, Pastor. I just can't believe you're a sinner. Not you."

"I'm sorry to disappoint you, Judi, but I am."

I returned to the rainbow arrangement, but it wasn't fun anymore. All of the colors looked dull. My 14-year-old world was shattered. Pastor Rogahn was a sinner. I couldn't believe it. I didn't *want* to believe it. Anybody, everybody—but not him. He was perfect, flawless in my eyes. I couldn't look at him anymore. There he was wearing a pastoral collar, and he was a sinner.

I eventually came to terms with the fact that Pastor Rogahn was a sinner—that he wasn't perfect—and I was able to accept him despite his flaws and imperfections, except on those days when he wore his clerical collar. I don't know what it is about that collar, but whenever I see a pastor or priest wearing his clerical collar, I have a difficult time imagining him being a sinner. I imagine that's why some priests are fighting so hard to wear their collars during the sex scandal trials.

NINTH GRADE

GOSSIP

I had recently started the ninth grade and was trying to make the adjustment from a small Lutheran grade school to a large, inner city public high school. Pastor Rogahn frequently asked me about my classes, teachers, and friends. I was busy dusting his bookshelves one afternoon in October while he was at his desk working. He finally asked me how everything was going at school, which gave me the opportunity to tell him the rumor I'd been bursting to tell about one of my teachers. He cut me off in the middle of the story before I could even get to the good part.

"I want to share with you what I've learned about gossip, Judi," he said, turning around in his chair to face me. "I've found that when someone gossips about another person, I learn more about the person who is doing the gossiping than I learn about the person they are gossiping about."

My heart dropped down to my stomach. I felt really bad and wished I hadn't told him. I wondered what he had just learned about me. I was sure it wasn't good. I decided to try to defend myself.

"I wasn't really gossiping, Pastor. I was just telling you about a rumor I'd heard."

"I would consider that gossip," he said. "Let me ask you this, do you know if the rumor is true?" He was sitting with his legs apart and his hands on his knees, looking very confrontational.

"No."

"Well, how well do you know the person who told you the rumor?"

"Real well. I talk to her every day in English. She sits right across from me," I said, as I stood at the table next to the bookshelves and kept nervously opening and closing the cover on one of his books.

"So you've known her for all of about six weeks. She's your close, intimate friend. You know everything about her. Is she a Christian?"

"I don't know," I admitted, shrugging my shoulders.

"What about the person she heard the rumor from? Do you know who that person is?"

"Yes," I answered confidently.

"How well do you know him or her?" he asked, as he adjusted his glasses.

"Not very well, but I've seen her around."

"And do you know who she heard the rumor from?"

"No."

"So you don't know who started this rumor or whether it's true or not. Am I understanding you correctly?" He relaxed back in the chair, crossed his legs, and folded his arms across his chest.

I didn't want to answer him. I knew where he was going with this, and I had no way out. I decided to just apologize.

"Pastor, I'm sorry," I said, as I stared at the floor and sunk my hands deeper into my pants pockets. "I was really just trying to make conversation with you, and I thought the rumor would be interesting to talk about. I hope you didn't learn something bad about me."

I looked at him for some sign that he wasn't mad at me. He stroked his chin and thought about it for a minute.

"When someone passes on gossip to me, I usually try to understand what their motive might be," he said. "You tell me your motive was to make conversation. So what did I learn about you? I learned that you're willing to repeat a rumor you don't know to be true just to make conversation."

"It sounds bad when you say it like that," I said, using my dust rag to wipe off the table since I hadn't been dusting his bookshelves since we began this conversation.

"It is bad. Suppose the rumor isn't true, Judi? How would you like it if someone passed on a rumor about you just to make conversation? Jesus doesn't like gossip. He doesn't want us to spread rumors about people. But Satan does. Why? Because Satan is the Father of Lies, the Great Deceiver. He loves to worm his way into people's lives through rumors and gossip.

"And he tries to do it in some unsuspecting ways. One is through teenagers like you. Another way that might surprise you is through prayer. Well, maybe not actually prayer, but through prayer groups. Prayer groups need to be careful that they don't turn into a forum for gossip."

"Why would someone want to gossip to God?" I wondered out loud.

"They wouldn't," Pastor Rogahn said. "They want to gossip to another person, and they do it in the form of a prayer request. To give you an example, let's say a church member here at Messiah approaches another church member to ask that she pray for her friend. She might even add that her friend is going through a difficult time and needs God's guidance and direction. That would be a prayer request.

"But suppose she continues by saying, 'My friend is going through a divorce. Her husband has been unfaithful, and she's having a terrible time of it. Please pray for her.' Her prayer request has become gossip. Is she telling this fellow member about her friend because she genuinely wants prayers for her friend, or is she just wanting to pass on gossip?

"Satan loves to watch gossip disguise itself in the form of a prayer request, and he also likes to use people to solicit gossip. People will come up to me and say, 'What's going on with so and so? I'd like to pray for them.' And I have to consider who the person is who is doing the asking and what their motive is to determine whether they are interested in praying for the person or just interested in hearing some juicy gossip."

I had never really thought of gossip as being that big of a sin before. Heck, it wasn't even a commandment. It wasn't on God's top-ten list, or so I thought.

"If gossip is such a terrible sin, Pastor, then why didn't God make it a commandment not to gossip?"

"He did," he replied. "What's the eighth commandment?"

"Thou shalt not bear false witness against thy neighbor," I answered without hesitation, pleased with myself that I had remembered something from my confirmation classes, "not thou shalt not gossip."

"And when your class talked about this commandment with Mr. Buckert, what did you decide bearing false witness means?" he asked me.

I couldn't remember. He walked over by me to the bookshelves and pulled down a gold hardback copy of *Luther's Small Catechism*. He opened it and started reading. "Here it is, on page five, Luther says, 'We should fear and love God that we may not deceitfully belie, betray, slander, nor defame our neighbor, but defend him, speak well of him, and put the best construction on everything.'"

He closed the book. "Gossiping and spreading rumors are forms of bearing false witness," Pastor Rogahn explained. "So as a Christian I would think you would want to refrain from listening to or repeating gossip. I know I do."

He put Luther's book back on the shelf and returned to his desk, picked up a pen and started writing. I don't know if his lecture to me had given him an idea for a sermon or if all our talking had made him realize he had better get to work before the afternoon disappeared. I started removing some books from the shelves so I could finish dusting.

As I worked, I thought about Pastor Rogahn's lecture on gossip. The rumor about the teacher that I couldn't wait to share with him earlier suddenly seemed insignificant. I wondered why I had wanted to tell the rumor to him in the first place. I never told it to anyone else.

CREATION

Pastor Rogahn was rummaging through his desk drawers, pulling out stacks of papers and other items and placing them on his desk. I didn't know what he was searching for, and I didn't ask. I was busy arranging his books by colors, with all the black ones first. I started with his ten-volume set of *Ancient Christian Commentary on Scripture.* He must have found what he was looking for because he stopped fumbling around and relaxed for a moment.

"How's school going?" he asked.

"Okay, I guess. I'll probably flunk science, though."

"Why do you say that?"

"Because I got in a debate with Dr. Washington about his big bang theory, and it ended in a stalemate."

"It's not Dr. Washington's theory, Judi. And I assume you told him that God created the world, which I'm sure he's already heard. Then what happened?"

"He told me I could believe and accept both theories. He said I could believe God created the big bang, and then everything evolved from there—all the plant and animal life and people."

"He's wrong, Judi. What he told you is totally inaccurate. He doesn't know what he's talking about."

"He's a doctor," I protested. "He's really smart. There are only a couple of teachers at school who are doctors, and he's one of them."

I picked up a black book titled, *Design for Preaching*, and placed it with the others on the second shelf.

"I don't care who he is; he's wrong. And he isn't a medical doctor. He most likely has a doctorate of philosophy in science, and he's not that smart. If he'd open up his Bible once in awhile, instead of a science journal, he'd read in the very first sentence that 'In the beginning *God* created the heavens and the earth.' It doesn't say God created a big bang, and then we all evolved. Don't cast aside everything you learned at Messiah because of the misguided opinion of a teacher with 'doctor' in front of his name. What about the opinion of someone with 'pastor' in front of his name? Or better yet, what about God's opinion?"

"I know God's responsible for creation, Pastor. That's why I had the debate with Dr. Washington. I was just a little confused about whether God caused the big bang or not, that's all. Dr. Washington threw me off with that one."

"The first and second chapters of Genesis are quite explicit in explaining creation. Perhaps you should give them another reading. Plants, animals, and man did not evolve from water molecules or from a big bang. They were created by God. You learned that way back in the first grade. Do you need to relearn it now in the ninth grade? Anytime anyone tells you something that goes against what God has to say, you should question it. When in doubt, go with God."

Dr. Washington told me I didn't have to believe the big bang theory; I just had to know it. I read the first couple chapters of Genesis again and chose to accept the opinion of the teacher with "pastor" in front of his name.

RELIGION

Pastor Rogahn was talking on the phone. He smiled and motioned for me to take a seat. I sat down and opened my literature book, hoping to catch up on some homework. I hadn't even finished answering the first question when he hung up and walked over to greet me.

"Hi, old friend," he smiled. "I've been thinking about my bookshelves (as if he ever thought of anything else), and I think they'd look nice if all my 'the' books came first."

"Huh?" was all I could muster.

"My 'the' books, Judi. All my books that begin with the word 'the' like *The Word of the Lord Grows* and *The Theology of Post-Reformation Lutheranism*. You wouldn't have to arrange them in alphabetical order, but I sure would like to see how my shelves would look with all my 'the' books first."

He stood there with his hands on his hips, smiling, thinking about how his shelves would look arranged with his "the" books first, and he looked deliriously happy. I thought it sounded like a goofy arrangement, but I didn't want to burst his bubble.

"At least you'll be able to find all your 'the' books when you need them," I said. "I bet you'll love it, Pastor."

"I bet I will," he said, still grinning. "Let's try it."

I started removing all but those books that started with "the" from the first shelf. Pastor Rogahn went back to his desk.

"I'm glad you came to church Sunday," he said. "I haven't seen you for awhile. My books have been neglected."

"Sorry, Pastor," I apologized. "I spent the night with my friend Diane last week, and I went to church with her again at St. Pius."

"Oh, your Catholic girlfriend," he remembered. "Why don't you bring her to Messiah with you one Sunday and introduce her to your favorite pastor?"

"You're my only pastor," I reminded him, "and her mom won't let her come. She won't even let her spend the night with me on a Saturday. She won't let her go to any church that isn't Catholic. Diane says her mom thinks only Catholics are going to heaven. Diane doesn't believe that, but she still can't come. Where did her mom get such a goofy idea? It doesn't say that in the Bible, does it?"

I started clearing off the shelves in the last two sections so I could place some of "the" books that were accumulating on the table.

"If it did, I would have been a priest," Pastor Rogahn said. "It's just another myth, Judi. Not all Catholics buy into that myth. But Catholics aren't the only group of Christians who think they're going to be alone in heaven. There are some Lutherans who believe they're the only group who's going, some Baptists think they'll be the only ones there, some Pentecostals, and so on and so forth."

"I guess we won't know until we get there, right, Pastor?" I asked, not really needing or expecting an answer.

"Wrong, Judi, we do know who's going to be there when we get there: everyone who believes that Jesus Christ is the Son of God. What does John 3:16 tell us? 'For God so loved the world that He gave His only begotten Son that whosoever believes in Him shall not perish but have everlasting life.' That's who's going to be there. . .whosoever. It doesn't matter if they're Catholic, Lutheran, Baptist, Pentecostal, or whosoever. If they have faith in Jesus Christ, they'll be there."

"Pastor, why do we have so many different religions if we all believe in Jesus Christ? Why don't we all just worship together? Why can't Diane come to our church?"

"You and Diane *are* the same religion, Judi. You're both Christians. If she were Muslim, Buddhist, Jewish, or some other non-Christian religion, then she would be a different religion. We have so many different sects of Christianity because we interpret God's Word differently. Some groups of Christians don't believe in baptizing infants, while others do. Some Christians, we, for example, believe Jesus is actually present in the wafer and wine at communion. Other Christians, Baptists, for instance, believe the bread and wine only symbolize Jesus, that He is not actually present."

"That's why we can't worship together even though we're all Christians," I surmised.

"Exactly," he said. "But Jesus says, 'My body is broken.' His body being the church, of course. He would love to see all us Christians get back together at some point. We're all going to be together in heaven."

"Boy, is Diane's mom going to be surprised when she sees us there," I said. "But, Pastor, do you think all us Christians will ever get back together again and worship together?"

"That would be nice," he said, "but I don't see it happening in my lifetime and probably not in yours, either. We just have too many differences that can't be ironed out. We Lutherans can't even agree among ourselves; we've branched off into different sects. I don't know how we could compromise with other Christian groups when we can't reach an agreement ourselves. The body is broken."

I stopped attending church with Diane. I reasoned that if her mom wouldn't let her attend my church, then I wasn't going to her church either.

Pastor Rogahn has influenced my views of other Christian religions. Although I have remained Lutheran and have married a Lutheran husband, we have found a Pentecostal church that we enjoy attending occasionally.

Recently, a family member told me I need to raise my children to be good Lutherans. I said, "I don't think so. I want to raise them to be good Christians. Is it more important for them to follow denominational traditions or the teachings of Jesus Christ?" She misunderstood me, thinking I meant I wasn't going to raise them in the Lutheran church. She was upset by my statement. I think she and Diane's mom are going to be surprised to see each other in heaven.

POLITICS

I sneaked up on Pastor Rogahn and peered over his shoulder. He was writing a letter.

"Hi, Pastor. What are you doing?"

"Writing a thank-you note. What are *you* doing?"

"Watching you write a thank-you note. I think you need a comma after gift." I pointed to the word in his letter, and he swatted my hand.

"Always the English student. How are your other classes going?"

"Mr. Rosenthal is still getting on my nerves. He's still making us clip articles about the bicentennial, and we celebrated it three months ago. Some kid brought up the election today, though, and we talked about that. What do you want me to do with your books, anyway? I forgot to ask."

"We haven't dusted in awhile. Why don't we dust today?"

I got the dust rag and glass cleaner from the bottom filing cabinet drawer and got to work. Pastor Rogahn resumed his letter writing. I had dusted only one shelf when I interrupted him again.

"Pastor, who are you gonna vote for?"

He jotted down a few more words and then answered me. "Who are you going to vote for?"

"Very funny, Pastor."

"If they passed a law tomorrow allowing 14 year olds to vote, who would you vote for?"

"Jimmy Carter."

"Why?"

"Because I don't like the president."

"Why?"

"Because he pardoned Nixon."

"You don't like Ford because he forgave Nixon. Was Nixon truly repentant for his sins?"

"I don't know, Pastor," I said. I took some more books off the shelves and laid them on the table. "I just don't like the guy."

"Nixon insisted he had done nothing wrong, so he probably wasn't truly repentant. Should Ford have pardoned him? What would Jesus have done? Would Jesus have forgiven him and told him to go and sin no more? Or would he have said, 'This man refuses to listen even to the church; treat him as a tax collector?'"

"I don't know, Pastor. What does it matter? Jesus can't vote."

"Let's talk about the candidate you do like—Jimmy Carter. Why would you vote for him? What do you like about him?"

"He just seems more like a real guy, and since I don't like Ford, I'd vote for Carter. You still haven't told me who you're gonna vote for."

"Who do you think Jesus would vote for?"

"I don't know, and I don't care. Jesus can't vote anymore than I can. But you can, Pastor."

"I don't know who I'm going to vote for yet. I'm going to study the backgrounds and platforms of both candidates and try to decide if Jesus were going to vote in this election, who He would vote for. Then I'll cast my ballot for that man."

I let it drop. All I wanted to know was who he was going to vote for in the election. He never told me before or after he had cast his ballot.

Student Senate elections rolled around a few months after my discussion with Pastor Rogahn. I selected the candidate I thought Jesus would most likely choose.

Snow

I met Pastor Rogahn coming up the steps to church. He pulled his hat down lower to try to cover his ears. The first snow of the year was falling hard with about two inches covering the ground. I had to run to keep up with him.

"Where ya been?" I asked.

"Making hospital visits," he said, as he opened the door for me and then scurried in behind me. "You're early. You didn't cut your last class again, did you?" He gave me his best attempt at a parental frown.

"No, they let us out early 'cause of the snow."

We stepped inside his office, removed our coats and hats and hung them on the corner rack. Pastor Rogahn removed a handkerchief from his back pocket and wiped the snow splatter from his glasses.

"Isn't it great, Pastor? They say we're supposed to get six to eight inches. They'll probably cancel school tomorrow. Don't you just love snow? I do. I hope we get a whole foot of snow, don't you? Wouldn't that be great?"

"Is it the snow you love or the thought of school being canceled?" he asked.

I didn't even have to think about it. "Both," I said. "If school gets canceled, I could go over to Art Hill and ride my sled. A bunch of kids had a snowball fight on the way home from school today. It was really fun. There's a lot of stuff you can do when it snows that you can't do otherwise, Pastor."

"And there are a lot of things you *have* to do when it snows that you wouldn't have to do otherwise, like shovel your walk, clean off your car, and drive in the snow. . ."

He walked over to his desk and sat down as if he were ending the conversation, but I wouldn't let it go.

"I don't have to do any of those things, Pastor. I love snow. Anyway, didn't God give us snow? Shouldn't we thank Him for it like we do everything else?"

Pastor Rogahn laughed. "Who's the pastor and who's the fourteen year old in the room?"

"You're the pastor," I said.

"That's what I thought. You had me wondering for a minute, Judi. But you're right. I guess I forgot how much fun snow can be. I've been grumbling and complaining about it instead of expressing my appreciation to God. I'm sure my ten-year-old son feels the same way you do, so I bet I'll be doing some sledding tomorrow. On behalf of David, I thank God for snow."

"Thank God for snow," I echoed, "and, Pastor, thank God for sleds."

"Thank God for sleds," agreed the pastor who ten minutes ago was complaining about snow.

CHRISTMAS

Pastor Rogahn wanted his books in a festive arrangement today. Since it was the Christmas holiday season, he thought his bookshelves would look nice if I alternated the red and green books. I told him it wouldn't work. He had a lot of red books, but there just weren't enough green books. He decided that when I ran out of green books, I should alternate with red and gold, then red and white, red and blue, and so on.

This was going to be one of the more complicated and time-consuming arrangements. I had started clearing all but the red books off the first shelf when his secretary came into the office with the mail.

"Where do you want me to put all these Christmas cards?" she asked him. "I've already covered the office door, the counter, and the bulletin board. I've run out of space for them."

"You can just leave them on my desk for now," he told her. "We'll find a place for them."

She did as he asked, seeming relieved to be free of the responsibility. I stared at the pile of cards on his desk. I couldn't think of any other holiday when people sent as many cards as they did at Christmas. I knew my parents always got lots of Christmas cards, but we never got cards at Thanksgiving or Easter or any of the other holidays.

"Pastor, Christmas is the most important holiday of the year because that's when Jesus was born, right?" I asked, trying to impress him with my theological insight. "That's why everyone sends cards at Christmas and not at other holidays, right?"

"Christmas is an important holiday, Judi," he said, "but, no, I wouldn't say it's the *most* important holiday. It's not the most important event Christians celebrate. There are those who aren't Christians who are willing to admit that Jesus was born. His life is too well documented to deny that. It's great that God sent us a Son, but Jesus' birth isn't the most important holiday to Christians. What do you suppose would be the most important holiday to us?"

I thought for a long time. I couldn't think of another holiday on which we sent as many cards as Christmas. Then it came to me.

"I know what it is. It's Good Friday," I said with confidence, hoping the pastor would be impressed that I'd remembered something from my confirmation classes. "That's when Jesus died for our sins. That's the most important holiday."

"No," Pastor Rogahn said, "it isn't. In fact, I wouldn't consider Good Friday a holiday at all. What's good about it? Jesus was whipped and beaten and nailed to a cross, and then He died. It was a sad day. There's no celebration there. No trumpets to blow. No banners to wave. No cards to be sent. Jesus died. He died, and He was buried. But what happened three days later?"

"He arose from the dead," I said.

"Sound the trumpets! Jesus is alive!" Pastor Rogahn shouted, raising a fist into the air. "Easter is the most important holiday to Christians, Judi. So what if Jesus was born? So what if He died? But He arose from the dead. He's alive and well. Now that calls for a celebration. Jesus is alive. We can talk to Him anytime we want to."

"Pastor, if Easter is so important, then why does everyone make such a big deal about Christmas? Why don't we send cards and give presents at Easter instead of at Christmas?"

"Tradition," he explained. "People do things year after year after year because their parents did it before them, and their parents before them and so on. And there isn't anything wrong with giving and receiving presents, but we need to remember that Christmas is Jesus' birthday and celebrate it as a Christian holiday. It was the day God sent us our Savior."

"So it is an important holiday," I said, satisfied that he had finally agreed with me.

"Yes, Judi, it's an important holiday. But it's not the most important holiday."

Included in Pastor Rogahn's Holy Night sermon was his own adaptation of Clement C. Moore's poem, "The Night Before Christmas." After many requests, he had it printed in the Messiah church newsletter "with apologies to the author."

'Twas the night before Christmas when all through
    the church,
Not a creature was stirring, no hunting, no search.
The trees and the trimmings were put up with care
(As if decorations meant God would come there!)
Most children were nestled at home in their beds,

Their parents were tired, some holding their heads.
A few came with kerchiefs, one had a new cap,
But all settled back for a long sermon's nap.
When up in the pulpit there came verbal clatter,
And people sat up to see what was the matter:
"Did somebody faint?" "Did the big tree go crash!?"
Or had the time come to start offering up cash?
The darkness around made it frightening to some,
And people sat waiting to see what was to come.
Then, what to my wondering eyes should appear
But a preacher all joyful and ready to cheer;
Of medium age and reasonably tall
(Some people imagined it might be St. Paul.)
More rapid than eagles his words swiftly came,
And it seemed he was calling us all by our name:
"Now, Billy! Now, Donald! Now, Mary and Su!
On, Alice! On, Barbara! On, David! On, You!
To the coming new year, to the days yet to be,
Let's move it! Let's do it! It takes you and me!
As new plants that out of the good ground can grow,
And after they're nourished, are ready to go,
Convinced, by his words, there was work to be
        done.
When (just for a second) I thought I could hear
The whining and sighing of hearts filled with fear,
As I pulled back with doubt and was going to
        snooze,
Down to ME came this figure, full of good news.
He was dressed in his robes, as they do at a service,
And his manner convinced me I need not be nervous.
"I'm always with you" was the message He had,
And I knew that it couldn't mean anything bad.
His eyes how they sparkled! His smile reassuring.
His face looked content like a cat when it's purring.
His mouth was declaring a wonderful thing;

It seemed that my heart was ready to sing.
His voice was directed especially to me,
And promises came of great things yet to be.
He was truly dynamic! A heavenly man!
And that was the moment the puzzle began.
I looked and I thought, "Is that Pastor Rogahn?
Or, is Someone Else here?" And my mind rambled
      on—
"Do you suppose it could really be. . . .HIM?
The Son of the Father? And of the virgin?"
There wasn't a way I could prove it to any,
But the same experience seemed to happen to many.
We pondered for hours, as we each went our way,
Whether *Someone* was there, when God's word had
      been spoken,
And *Someone* had cast out a spell still unbroken,
The voice said it plainly, so believe if you choose,
"*God* has come here this Christmas!
And for all that's GOOD NEWS."

PARENTS

Tears were still running down my cheeks when I walked into Pastor Rogahn's office. He was working at his desk, so I went over to greet him.

"What's wrong with my best book tender?" he asked. "Did they pass a law saying you have to go to school year round?

"You're not funny, Pastor. And if you really want to know, everything's wrong. My dad's messed up my whole life. I can never go back to school again."

I wiped my nose on my sleeve. Pastor Rogahn stood up to reach across his desk for a box of tissues and offered one to me.

"Let's sit at the table," he suggested. "You can tell me all about it."

I told him what had happened the day before. A boy at school named Kenneth, who sat behind me in art class, had been hitting me and pulling my hair. He would do the same things when he'd see me in the halls. I had told my mother about it but told her not to worry, that I could handle it myself. She told my dad. He had stormed into the principal's office, cursing and demanding that the boy stop bullying me. Kenneth and I were both called into the office and had to listen to my dad rant and rave.

"That was embarrassing enough, Pastor, but then today I go to my art class, and the teacher starts jumping all over me. The principal talked to her and had Kenneth transferred to another class.

"She said, 'I never saw Kenneth do anything to you. Why didn't you tell *me* about it, you little snitch?'

"Pastor, I could've handled it myself. Why would my dad want to embarrass me like that? I'm never talking to him again."

The pastor was sitting with his legs crossed and his hands folded in his lap. He hadn't interrupted me once as I told my story.

"I'm sorry, Judi. I can understand why you would have been embarrassed, but let's look at the situation from your father's point of view. Do you think his intention was to embarrass you?"

"Yes."

"I don't think so. No parent intentionally sets out to embarrass his child, although I'm sure we all do sometimes without meaning to. Its sounds to me as though your father wanted to protect you from Kenneth and to keep you from getting hurt. Perhaps he could have gone about it in a different manner. It would have been nice if he had consulted you before going to the principal, but he didn't. Parents have an animal-like instinct to want to protect their offspring, and they may not always think things through when they believe their child is in danger."

"Why are you sticking up for him, Pastor? What he did was wrong, wasn't it?"

"Yes and no. His intention was to help you, but his behavior hurt you. It embarrassed you. He was out of control. He's not a perfect father, Judi. I'm not a perfect father. There's no such thing as a perfect earthly father. We all make mistakes. But you do have a perfect heavenly Father to turn to whenever you need Him. He never makes mistakes. He's always in control. He will never embarrass you. He's perfect in every way, and He loves you beyond measure."

"Pastor, I think David's really lucky to have you for a father."

"I'm sure he would disagree with you at times. I can be a slave driver." He stood up and clapped his hands together. "Come on now, let's get to work. These books aren't going to arrange themselves, you know."

Kenneth left me alone. He was a little immature, and his hitting me had been his attempt at showing affection. I eventually forgave my father for embarrassing me.

HEAVEN

I hadn't tended to the pastor's books for quite a few weeks because I hadn't been to church for him to ask me. He never called me at home. He always caught me in the receiving line after a Sunday service and asked me to stop by his office on a given afternoon.

I was arranging his books according to width today. All the skinny ones were to go on the top shelves with the big, bulky ones on the lower shelves. Pastor Rogahn was reorganizing his filing cabinet, getting rid of some old files he no longer needed. He had his trash can next to him, filled to the brim with papers, so he must have been at it for awhile.

"I haven't seen you in church in awhile, Judi," he said. "I was beginning to think I was going to have to start looking for someone else to tend to my books, and it's hard to find a good book tender these days."

"Church is boring," I said, as I took down his *Concordance to the Greek Testament* from the top shelf and set it on the table. "I just go every once in awhile so that I'll go to heaven, and so you can let me know when you want me to tend to your books."

"If you're going to church just to get to heaven, you're wasting your time," Pastor Rogahn said, as he pitched a wadded-up paper ball at the trash can and missed.

"There's only one way to get to heaven, Judi, and that's through faith alone in Jesus Christ. But you're not the only one who believes that myth. I'd say at least a third of the adults at Messiah attend church for the same reason you do, thinking it will get them into heaven." He bent down, picked up the paper ball, and tossed it into the can. I removed a dictionary from the upper shelf and placed it on the lower shelf.

"We attend church not to get to heaven," he said, "but to praise and glorify God. Everything we do in church is to glorify God. If you're not doing something to glorify God, then what's the point of doing it? If you're not singing that song to glorify God, then don't sing it. If you're not praying that prayer to glorify God, then don't pray it, because it's sure not going to get you to heaven.

"I suppose church *would* be pretty boring if you're going just to try to get to heaven, because that isn't the purpose of going to church. It wouldn't be any different than going to a baseball game just to try to get to heaven, because that isn't the purpose of going to a baseball game."

"I get what you're saying, Pastor, but one thing that bothers me is that a lot of people in that church are a lot older than me. I don't think it's fair if I start going to church every Sunday and glorifying God for the rest of my life and get to go to heaven, but some of those old people just start glorifying God now, and they get to go to heaven, too. Why should they get to go when I've been a Christian almost my whole life, and they just want to start being a Christian right before they die just so they can go to heaven? It doesn't seem fair to me."

He stood there with his left hand on his right elbow and his right hand on his chin, and he thought for a long time before he spoke.

"So you don't like it that someone can come in at the last minute and be saved?" he asked, without waiting for a reply. "You don't like it when you're waiting in line at the movie theater, and a guy comes later than you, gets in the line next to you, and his line moves faster. He moves ahead of you and gets his ticket first. You're angry. You waited longer. You're both going to see the same movie at the same time, but you had to wait longer. It's isn't fair!

"Do you understand the analogy, Judi?"

"No, we're not talking about going to a movie. We're talking about going to heaven," I reminded him.

"Everyone who buys a ticket gets to see the show," he explained. "Everyone who believes that Jesus is the Son of God has a ticket to meet Him on Judgment Day. It doesn't matter when you bought the ticket. It doesn't matter if you've waited six minutes or sixty years to meet Him. If you've got a ticket, you're going to the show. It's God's plan, and it's fair."

"I guess so," I said, still not really sure that God's plan was fair.

There were several times during my teenage years when I misplaced my ticket to the show and many more times as an adult when I was sure I had lost the ticket altogether. But I always found it again.

My father passed away on December 9, 2002. He was one of the guys at the movie theater who came in at the last minute, bought his ticket, and was saved. Now I think God's plan is fair.

I'll see you at the show, Daddy.

Youth Group

"I sure wouldn't want to be the new guy coming to Messiah's youth group," Pastor Rogahn said out of the blue.

He startled me. He hadn't spoken to me after giving me my assignment. He wanted his books arranged in alphabetical order by author. I was concentrating so hard on trying to find the rest of the authors whose last names started with the letter B that I'd forgotten he was even in the room.

"What are you talking about, Pastor?"

He was sitting at his desk, not doing anything as far as I could see.

"I'm talking about the sisters who joined your youth group. You know who I'm talking about, the two you were all making sport of in front of church the other evening."

He was talking about Linda and Christine, sisters who looked as though they had just stepped out of the 1950s. They were both about four-feet ten-inches tall. Linda had long, thin, stringy brown hair and weighed about 65 pounds. Her sister had a dark brown, curly do and still had most of her baby fat. They were both dressed in plaid skirts, knit sweaters, and penny loafers.

"You mean Linda and Christine, the Bobbsey Twins?" I laughed. "Come on, Pastor, we were just teasing them. You have to admit, they did look pretty silly. It was all in fun. They were laughing, too. What a couple of nerds they are."

"And what makes you better than them?"

"I don't dress like that, for one thing."

"You don't dress like that. So how do you dress? Let's see, today you're wearing a pair of jeans with a hole in the knee, a sweatshirt that's ten times too big for you, your dad's old army shirt, and a pair of worn-out sneakers. In my opinion, they dress better than you do. What else makes you better than them?"

"I don't know, Pastor. Why are you jumping all over me, anyway? I wasn't the only one making fun of them; everybody was."

"I know, Judi. I saw it, and I was very disappointed. Our youth group is supposed to be a Christian group, but it sure didn't look like one. The scene reminded me of the men who mocked and ridiculed Jesus before He died. Do you suppose the evening was fun for Linda and Christine?"

I hadn't really thought about it. I had just been engaging in group behavior, going along with what everybody else was doing. I guessed if I had been alone with them I would have treated them differently. Pastor Rogahn was getting to my conscience.

"I never really thought about it, Pastor. I guess it wasn't any fun for them. I'm sorry," I said.

"I believe you, and I forgive you. But I think the sisters are the ones you should apologize to and maybe make an effort to try to include them in the group next time rather than exclude them."

I never apologized to the sisters, but I did make an effort to include them in the group. Linda made a dramatic change. She changed her hairstyle and started wearing jeans and dressing like the gang. Unfortunately, she also, like many of us, started smoking. Christine changed for no one.

I ran into Christine about ten years ago at McDonald's. It was the first time I had seen her since youth group. I had gotten an order to go, but I saw her dining alone and joined her. She asked me to call her "Chris." I told her I had never noticed how beautiful she is. Her complexion is flawless, her face wrinkle free. She's absolutely beautiful inside and out. She told me Linda had died during childbirth, and not a day goes by that she doesn't miss her.

She asked me why I was always so kind to her and Linda when everyone else was so mean. I told her that I genuinely liked her, and I meant it. Chris, I pray to God that this book finds its way into your hands, so we can rekindle our friendship. I still have a lot to learn from you in my Christian walk.

I apologize to Randy, Cindy, Debbie, Peter, Donna, Clifford, and any other kids who I "made sport of" before my lecture from Pastor Rogahn. I wish he had reached me before I met you.

Bad Things

I was standing by the bookshelves, arguing with Pastor Rogahn about the book arrangement he wanted. I was sure I had already organized his shelves with all his collections or book sets first. I had done that two years ago when I had first started tending to his books, and he wasn't satisfied with it then. I don't know why he thought he'd like the arrangement any better now. Not that it mattered. I was convinced he was never going to be happy with any arrangement, which was fine with me, but I wasn't going to do the same arrangement twice. It was the principle of the thing. I stood my ground, and finally he gave in.

"Okay," he said, "you're sure I didn't like it?"

"You hated it," I reminded him. "It split up your colors too much, remember? Some of your reds were on top, some in the middle, some on the bottom. You absolutely hated it. I won't do it again."

"All right," he said, waving his hand at me as if he were dismissing me. "I really don't like having my colors split up. That was the problem with the alphabetical arrangement, wasn't it? All the colors were separated. Why don't we try arranging the shelves with all my gold books first? We haven't tried that yet, have we?"

"No, Pastor, that's one way we haven't tried yet. Maybe you'll like that."

"Maybe I will," he said.

We both knew he wouldn't. He walked back to his desk and sat down while I started pulling all his gold books off the shelves and setting them on the table. There weren't that many. They might take up all of a shelf and a half.

"Say, I almost forgot," Pastor Rogahn said as soon as he sat down, "how did your visit with your grandmother go this weekend?"

I had been looking forward for weeks to seeing my grandma. She used to live nearby, but since my aunt had gotten divorced, Grandma had moved to the county to live with her and help take care of her kids. I didn't get to see her very often anymore. She was my favorite person in the whole world. She had a way of making each of her grandkids feel like they were her favorite.

"We didn't go," I said. "Grandma's sick, and she's the most Christian person I know, too. I don't understand why God always makes bad things happen to good people. He should just make bad people get sick, not good people."

"Don't be mad at God, Judi," Pastor Rogahn said. "God didn't make your grandmother sick. But you do bring up an interesting question. Why does God allow bad things to happen to good people? Why would God allow your grandmother to be sick? Your grandma is a good person, a good Christian. Why would God allow her to suffer?"

"That's what I want to know," I said. "Why does she always have to get sick? God must have it in for her or something, and she never did anything wrong."

I started removing all the books from the first two shelves to make room for the gold books.

"Your grandma's a sinner, just like we all are," he said, "but why would God let a good person like her suffer? It's quite simple, actually. Because He wants to make her well. The sickness didn't come from God. Only good things come from God. Bad things like sickness come from Satan. God allows the devil to inflict illnesses on us so that we will turn to Him for healing. We can pray for your grandma and ask God to heal her, but God isn't the one who made her sick."

"That seems kind of silly to me," I said, "that God would let the devil make someone sick just so He could make them well. What's the point?"

"There's a story in the Bible about a man named Job," Pastor Rogahn said. "If you want to talk about why God would allow bad things to happen to good people, Job's the man we want to talk about. God allowed Satan to do everything to Job that you can think of. Satan took his home, his family, all of his animals, everything, and then afflicted him with painful sores."

"Why did God let Satan do all that stuff to Job if he was a good guy?" I asked.

"That's an important point," he replied. "*God let Satan do it.* God didn't do any of those things. Remember, only good things come from God. God allowed Job to suffer so that he could see how much he needed God, so that he would appreciate God so much more than he had before his suffering. He also allowed it to test Job's faith. When bad things happen to good people and they turn to God for help, they have a greater appreciation for God, for His divine power, His grace, and His love."

"So, Pastor, I can still get mad at God then for allowing Satan to make bad things happen to good people. If God wouldn't let him do it, then bad things wouldn't happen. So it's still God's fault."

"It isn't God's fault, Judi. It's God's right. God created us. Everything we have, we have because of Him, including our health. If He sees a need to let the devil have a go at us to strengthen our faith in Him, then that's what He'll do. We shouldn't question Him. He always has our best interests in mind. We should just turn to Him in prayer and in faith and ask that His will be done. If you always remember that only good things come from God, then you can trust that His will is going to be what is best for you."

"So if I pray for Grandma to get well, and only good things come from God, then God should make her well," I reasoned.

"God can heal, and He wants to make her well, but on His timetable, not yours. Keep praying for her, but pray also that God's will be done. God has Grandma's best interests at heart. He knows what He's doing, but we don't know what He's doing. Let's put Grandma in His hands."

"Okay, Pastor," I sighed. There was no use arguing with him. I knew I would never win a theological debate. I decided I would just keep praying for Grandma to get well.

Grandma recovered from a bout of the flu, and I visited with her a couple weeks later. I continued to pray for her health, and I'm sure Pastor Rogahn did, too.

Grandma never got sick again, not even so much as a cold. She died about a year and a half later, on January 2, 1978, of heart failure.

TENTH GRADE

Spiritual Gifts

I bounced into Pastor Rogahn's office with a smile plastered across my face that hadn't left since I got out of school that afternoon. He was standing to the side of the filing cabinet. He had the top drawer open, and a file folder was lying open across it as he was writing on a memo pad on top of the cabinet.

"I got it!" I said, jumping up and down in a circle. "I was hoping I would. I prayed that I would. You said you'd pray that I would, and I did. I got it!"

I was still grinning, and Pastor Rogahn was smiling now, too. "Got what?" he asked.

"Got what?! How could you forget already? I got my own column for the school paper, remember?"

"How could I forget something that important?" he said, tapping himself on the head with his pen. "Did you decide on a name for your column?"

"The class came up with the name. They always call me a pinhead, and since it's a humor column, we're gonna call it, "The Pinhead Speaks." How does that sound to you?"

He scratched his head and thought about it. "Well, I suppose if you like it, that's what matters."

"I like it," I said, with a nod of satisfaction. "At least right away everyone will know whose column it is just by the title."

"And have you thought about a topic for your first column yet?"

"Yep." I had hoisted myself up on the table and was swinging my legs back and forth as we talked. I just couldn't sit still. "I figured since we're in the middle of football season, I'd write about football. It would have to be something funny, though. What do you think?"

He closed the file folder, shut the drawer, leaned back against the filing cabinet, and folded his arms across his chest.

"I think you ought to write about Jesus," he said.

I stopped swinging my legs and sat still, looking at him for some indication that he was joking, but he held a poker face.

"I can't write about Jesus," I said. "First of all, Pastor, it's a public school. Second, it's a humor column. I'm gonna write about football."

"Jesus has a sense of humor," he said, "and so do I. I'm teasing you, of course. I think football sounds like a great idea for your first column. You can have some fun with it. Now, who are you going to write that first column for?"

"The students," I answered.

"No, you're not," he said. "Who are you really going to write that column for?"

I had taken journalism my freshman year, and now I was a sophomore taking a publications course and writing my own column. What did Pastor Rogahn think he was going to teach me about being a journalist? He was just a pastor, after all.

"The students are my primary target audience, Pastor," I sighed. "I'm going to write the column for them."

"No, you're not," he said. "You're going to write that column for Jesus."

I looked at him for some sign that he was teasing me again, but he didn't crack a smile.

"You're not going to write your column *about* Jesus, but you're going to write it *for* Jesus. Jesus is your primary target audience for everything you do. He's the one who gave you the gift of writing, not the students. So you want to glorify Him with your gift. You can still write about football if you want to. Just remember that Jesus gave you the gift to be able to write that column on football. He's your audience."

That made sense. I figured he was partially right. I knew my journalism teacher, Mr. Jackson, had said the students were my target audience, and now Pastor Rogahn was telling me that Jesus was my target audience. I decided I would combine the lessons of Mr. Jackson and Pastor Rogahn and write to both audiences.

"God gives each of us unique gifts and abilities," the pastor said. "It doesn't matter what spiritual gifts we have, whether it's teaching, preaching, writing, or whatever. We can use those gifts to the glory of God. Use your gift to the best of your ability, and don't forget to thank God for it. And, who knows, maybe someday you will decide you want to write about Jesus."

I did decide to write about Jesus a few months later. Mr. Jackson occasionally allowed me to write humorous poems in addition to my column. When Christmas rolled around, I found I was able to write about Jesus for a public school newspaper without mentioning His name. Pastor Rogahn was pleased with how I had developed and used my spiritual gift.

I only wish he could see this book.

HONOR

"Why don't we put God first today, Judi?" Pastor Rogahn said. "Let's arrange my books with those that have God or Jesus in the titles first. I think I'd really like that."

"I think you would, Pastor." It sounded like a great idea, this Jesus arrangement, one that might work for him. I scanned the shelves looking for titles and began pulling books that met the requirement. Pastor Rogahn walked over to the filing cabinet and started searching through the second drawer.

I immediately found a book with "Savior" in the title and asked the pastor if it counted as a Jesus book.

"I want anything that refers to Jesus in my Jesus arrangement," he said. "God, Jesus, Christ, Savior, Lord—I just want all my Jesus books in one spot on my shelves so I can find them easily."

It wasn't until I was editing this chapter when it struck me that Pastor Rogahn and I had a Jesus arrangement. I arranged his books for him, and he talked to me about Jesus. It was the perfect arrangement.

"How's everything in the life of Judi Hayes?" he asked, pulling a file from the drawer and taking it to his desk.

"Everything's boring at school, as usual, and tense at home, as usual."

"What's going on at home now?"

"Dad told Kevin to take his bastard kid and get out of his house, so Kevin punched him, and now Dad's in one of his moods. I've just been trying to stay out of his way."

My brother Kevin, seven years my senior, had been living at home, a requirement of the courts when he obtained custody of his daughter Dawn who was four when this incident happened.

"Pastor, when God made that commandment to honor your father and mother, he didn't mean fathers like my dad, did He? When Dad called Dawnie a name, didn't Kevin have the right to hit him? Look at all the times Dad beat up Kevin. He had it coming to him, didn't he?"

"Maybe he did, Judi. But that's not for me to decide or for you or Kevin to decide, either. The fourth commandment says we should honor our father and mother, which means we shouldn't provoke them to anger, but serve and obey them and hold them in love and esteem. I don't know what led up to your father's decision to ask Kevin and his child to leave. Did Kevin break one of the house rules or something?"

"I don't know, Pastor. I missed that part. He probably didn't do anything. You know how my dad gets sometimes when he's drinking."

"We'll pray for both of them to forgive each other. According to the Bible, you and Kevin do need to honor your father, no matter what kind of father he is. But God also says in Ephesians, 'Fathers, do not provoke your children to anger, but bring them up in the discipline and instruction of the Lord.' So God also wants your father to respect you and your siblings. Parents must love and cherish their children, or their children will become discouraged as Kevin has. Does he have a place to stay?"

"Yeah, he's moving in with his girlfriend."

"Let's see, with Kevin gone, John away at college, Karen married, and your other brother—what's his name?"

"Bob."

". . .Bob in the marines, you should be happy. You probably have your choice of bedrooms now."

"I'm still in the room I used to share with Karen. I don't want to move all my stuff. I like John's room, and he's home only during the summer and on holidays, but he won't give it up. Mom and Dad are talking about moving, anyway."

"Am I going to lose my book tender?"

"I won't know until I see where they move, Pastor."

Dad and Kevin eventually forgave each other. It was the second and last time Kevin ever struck my father. (He rejected some of my father's Lutheran teachings and is studying to be a Baptist minister.)

This is what my brother Kevin had to say about this incident:

The first time I ever hit my father he was drunk. I was 14 and had stayed out past curfew.

Dad said, "If you're gonna act like a man, I'm gonna beat you like a man." He punched me in the face.

"I don't want to fight you, Dad." He punched me in the face again. I said again, "I don't want to fight you, Dad." He punched me in the face again. This went on for several punches.

Finally he kicked me between the legs, and I fell on my hands and knees on the sidewalk. I came up swinging. I knocked him to the ground and was sitting on top of him, punching him in the face. I grabbed a brick that was lying nearby and brought my arm back to smash him over the head with it when a neighbor grabbed my arm. I probably would have killed him if she hadn't stopped me.

I came downstairs later that evening, and my father was sitting at the kitchen table. He had one hand soaking in peroxide and the other wrapped in an ice pack. I heard him tell my mother, "That boy ain't gonna take too many whippin's." I felt a sense of pride. It was the first time I had ever heard my father boast about me.

In the incident described in this chapter, I had gotten in an argument with my father because I needed him to co-sign on an application for a car. I had been working side by side at Chapman's Ice Cream with him for three years, yet he had called me a lazy, no-good bum, refusing to sign the form. He said, "If you don't like it, you can take your bastard kid and get the hell out of my house."

His comments about me were bad enough, but when he insulted my daughter, something inside of me snapped. He was sitting in his favorite chair that no one else was allowed to sit in. I punched him in the face, and both he and the chair toppled over backwards. Then I picked up the chair and hit him with it again and again and again, until all the legs had broken off the chair.

What I did was wrong. I didn't honor my father. When I was younger, I begged my mother to divorce him, but she was stuck. She had five kids and no job skills. There were so many nights as a child when I prayed to God for my father to die. I prayed something would happen to him at work or that he'd get killed driving home drunk, anything. I just wanted him to die. I began trying to patch things up with him around 1986, when I met and married a Christian woman. Dad mellowed out when he gave up alcohol in his fifties and even more so after his stroke in 1996.

He was diagnosed with cancer in July 2001. In December 2002 he was lying on his death bed, and I began praying for him to live. I was trying to say as many prayers as I could to cancel all the prayers I had said as a kid begging God to take his life. Dad died at age 76. I'm sorry, Dad. I love you, and I forgive you.

It's hard to honor a father who's an abusive, angry alcoholic. But when I became a Christian in 1994, I gained a better understanding of what "honoring thy father" meant. In the weeks before my father's death, I had the opportunity to lead him to the Lord. To me that was a great honor.

Prodigal Son

Pastor Rogahn wanted his books arranged with all the red ones first. He had a lot of them, especially with his collection of *Luther's Works*. I started with those. I had filled the first two shelves and added a red Bible and dictionary when his secretary came in and set two new phone books on his desk.

"We got our new phone books this week, too, Pastor," I said. "I called all the Richard Hayes in the book again, but none of them were my brother."

Richard was my father's son from his first marriage. I'd never met him. He was twelve years older than I was, and my father had stopped seeing him when he was seven. Richard had called when he had turned eighteen and had talked to my mother. He had informed her that he was joining the navy, and my father could stop sending child support payments. No one had heard from him since.

"The prodigal son," Pastor Rogahn said. "I'm sure you'll get to meet him someday, Judi. Keep praying for him to forgive your father. I'm sure he will someday."

"But what about Dad? What if the prodigal son does come home? We're not even allowed to mention Richard's name around Dad. Everything I know about him I got from my mom. I don't think it's going to be like in the Bible where the father welcomes him back with open arms and everything's okay."

I had finished with the red books and had started pulling all the blue books from the shelves to place next.

"Pray for God to soften your father's heart. I'm sure he wants to see his son again. I'll bet he's carrying a lot of guilt and has many regrets about his relationship with Richard. It's on God's timetable, not yours. When the time is right, the prodigal son and his father will reunite, and your father *will* welcome him with open arms."

"If you say so, Pastor. But I'm still going to try to find him. He probably doesn't even know he has any sisters."

"You'll find him when God's ready for you to find him."

I never did find Richard. He found me, my dad, and the whole family in 1996 when he was 47. It had been forty years since he'd last seen my father. My dad received a Father's Day card that read, "Dear Dad, I know it's been many years, but I'd like to bridge the gap." It was signed by Richard and included a phone number. He was living in Canton, Georgia, with his wife Joyce.

Richard came to St. Louis, and my father welcomed him with open arms, embracing him, and then his wife, in a warm hug. My father told Richard many times that he loved him, and they caught up on the last forty years.

Richard and Joyce are very much a part of the family now. He has since moved to Kansas City. He is a talented singer who, along with my brother Kevin, sang at my wedding.

LOVE

I peered into the box that someone had left on the table in Pastor Rogahn's office. It was full of blank index cards. I was wondering what he was going to do with all those cards. Just then he came waltzing into his office, humming, "Jesus loves me."

"I see you found my bookmarks," he said, reaching into the box and pulling out a handful of the cards.

"Bookmarks, huh?" I said, reaching in for some myself. "That's funny, I have some index cards at home that look exactly like your bookmarks."

"Well, now I have some bookmarks that look exactly like your index cards, Miss Smarty Pants," he said, holding some index cards up in each hand as if he were posing for a commercial. "And you are going to have the very distinct honor of placing one of these bookmarks in each my books."

"Why would you need a bookmark in every one of your books? You can't be reading all those books at the same time. You're just kidding, right?" I laughed.

He set the index cards he was holding on the table. "No, I'm not kidding. It's very frustrating to me when I'm reading a book and the phone rings or someone walks into my office, and I can't find a bookmark right away. So I decided I would just keep bookmarks in all my books. And since you're my book tender, placing the bookmarks would fall under your job description. If there aren't enough, just let me know."

He was serious. I don't know why I had questioned him. I mean, we're talking about a man who constantly wants his books rearranged, so why shouldn't he want bookmarks in all of his books? I guess he was finally satisfied with the arrangement where all his red books came first. But he was still obsessed with his books, and I was still getting paid a dollar per job.

He had retreated to his desk, and I had just inserted the fourth index card when he asked me how my friend Becky was doing. Becky and I had been confirmed at and had graduated from Messiah together and had then gone on to different high schools. When I last tended to the pastor's books, I had told him Becky was pregnant, that she was going to have the baby, but I didn't know if she was going to marry the baby's father or not.

"She's not getting married," I said, "and I'm glad. Having a baby's not a good reason for two people to get married anyway."

I didn't really know if it was or it wasn't. I was just repeating what I'd heard adults say.

"I'd have to disagree with you, Judi," Pastor Rogahn said. "I would say having a baby is a very good reason to get married. In fact, I would even go so far as to say it's one of the better reasons. But do you know what a bad reason is for couples to get married, perhaps even the worst reason?"

"No," I replied. I wasn't even going to try to venture a guess since I was way off on the baby thing.

"The worst reason for a couple to marry is because they're 'in love,'" he said. He was sitting back in his chair with both hands resting on his desk, palms down. He looked serious.

I didn't say a word. I had learned with Pastor Rogahn that when he made a shocking statement, there was always more to follow.

"That's right," he said, "because they are 'in love.' Couples come in to see me all the time and tell me they'd like to get married. I ask them why, and they say because they love each other. A few years later those same couples are back in my office again, telling me they would like to get divorced. I ask them why, and they say it's because they don't love each other anymore."

"Do you tell them that maybe they should have a baby?" I asked, as I inserted another index card between the pages of a book.

"No, having a baby is a good reason to *get* married," he said, "but we're not talking about getting married. We're talking about a couple who is already married but now want to separate because they don't love each other anymore.

"There is no such thing as perfect love in man's world. Our love for each other is marred with imperfections. What we call 'being in love' is a selfish love. It is impatient, envious, and self-serving," he said, counting the ways on his fingers, "the exact opposite of what Paul tells us it should be in I Corinthians. The only perfect love that exists is the love Jesus has for us. God loves us no matter what, not just when we make Him feel good. No other kind of love can be perfectly right or perfectly wrong. So couples who get married simply because they are in love are just setting themselves up for disappointment and failure."

"That doesn't make sense," I said. "You're saying someone should marry a person they don't love just so they won't be disappointed when they find out their love isn't perfect."

"No, what I'm saying is that someone should have a better reason for wanting to spend a lifetime with their partner other than that they're in love with the person. I'm actually considering not marrying any couples who can't give me at least one valid reason for why they want to spend their lives together other than that they love each other, because I don't want to see them back in my office again when they decide they don't love each other anymore."

"But Pastor," I said, "if you do that, you probably won't be marrying too many couples. I bet *most* people get married because they're in love."

"Exactly!" he said, tapping his fist on the desk in mock anger. "And that's why there are so many divorces."

"Because they don't love each other anymore," I said, completing his sentence for him. I felt like we were going around in circles.

"Perfect love," he sighed, "everyone wants that perfect love, and they can have it, too. They're just not going to get it from a spouse, or a parent, or a child, or anyone else other than Jesus. He has the only perfect love to give. All we have to do is accept it. That's all, just accept it. God loves us so much that He gave His Son to die for us. That's perfect love. Why is that so hard for people to understand and accept?"

"I don't know," I said, remaining as confused as I had been at the start of this conversation.

I really didn't understand all this perfect love stuff. Pastor Rogahn sure seemed to have some funny ideas. I wondered if he was serious about not marrying couples who were only marrying because they were in love. I decided right then that I would probably never get married, especially if I was supposed to marry someone that I didn't love.

I married a man in 1989 solely because we were in love. We divorced five years later when we discovered we didn't love each other anymore. It is interesting to note that our age difference was 28 years, the same as between Pastor Rogahn and me.

I married a Christian man in 1998 who has shown me God's kind of unconditional love. Now I know what Pastor Rogahn was talking about.

LENDING

I was dusting Pastor Rogahn's shelves when I came across a book that looked interesting to me. It was green and titled, *Pastoral Theology*. I started leafing through it, curious to know what Pastor Rogahn had studied to become a pastor. He caught me slacking on the job.

"Find something interesting, Judi?"

"Yeah, Pastor, could I borrow this book?" I held it up for him to see.

"You'd become bored with that book before you even finished the first chapter. Why would you want to read that?"

"I don't know," I said. "Just curious, I guess. I like the title."

"You can't judge a book by its cover. Besides, you've never returned the last book you borrowed from me. Or did you put it back on the shelf without telling me? I haven't seen it."

"It's at home, Pastor. I know right where it's at. I'll bring it back the next time I tend to your books."

"Did you read it?"

"I read a couple of pages. I just couldn't get into it. It wasn't what I expected it to be."

"And this book won't be what you expect it to be, either," he said. "It wasn't written for a fifteen year old.

You'll take it home, read a couple of pages and not return it."

"No, I won't. I promise," I begged. "I'll read the whole thing and bring both books back next time, and then we can talk about the book if you want to."

"I'll tell you what, Judi. I'm going to loan you the book, but sit down for a minute, please. I'd like to read something to you first."

He picked up his Bible and flipped it open. I sat down at the table, still clutching the book.

"Jesus says in the sixth chapter of Luke, 'And if you lend to those from whom you expect repayment, what credit is that to you? Even sinners lend to sinners expecting to be repaid in full. But love your enemies, do good to them, and lend to them without expecting to get anything back. Then your reward will be great, and you will be sons of the Most High, because He is kind to the ungrateful and wicked.'"

"What does all that mean, Pastor?"

"It means I'm loaning you the book, even though I'm fairly certain I'll never see it again, because that's what Jesus would do."

"Thanks, Pastor, and I'm going to return it because I'm fairly certain that's what Jesus would do."

Pastor Rogahn never hounded me about the books. I returned both to him a couple months later. I made several attempts at *Pastoral Theology* but never finished the first chapter. He never said, "I told you so." And I never asked to borrow another of his books.

QUESTIONS

Pastor Rogahn wanted his bookmarks personalized, bearing the title of the book in case a bookmark should become lost or misplaced. I had taken a stack of books to the table to work and had quickly tired of the job after writing out several long titles. I loathed the index cards and longed for the days of arranging his books. I was looking for a shortcut. Pastor Rogahn was reading at his desk when I interrupted him.

"Pastor, do I have to write out all these long titles, or can I just write down the key words?" I asked. "You'd still know which book it went to."

"What do you think, Judi?"

"I'm asking you."

"And I'm asking you, what do you suppose I'd want? What did I ask you to do?"

I was getting agitated. He wouldn't answer me.

"Pastor, why do you always answer my question with a question?"

"Do I do that?"

"You just did it again!"

"Did I?"

"Stop it, Pastor! You're not funny!"

"Jesus frequently answered a question with a question."

"Is that why you do it?"

"No, I hadn't thought about it until you mentioned it. But why do you suppose I would answer your questions with questions?"

"I don't know, maybe you don't know the answer, or maybe you're just trying to irritate me."

"Do you think I don't know the answer to the question you just asked me about my bookmarks? Why did Jesus always answer a question with a question? Was it because He didn't know the answer? Was it because He was trying to irritate His disciples or His followers?"

Pastor Rogahn picked up a small Bible that was lying on his desk and started paging through it. It only took him a couple of seconds to find what he was looking for.

"In the book of Luke, the first time Jesus speaks, it is to answer a question with a question. His parents had been searching for Him for three days. When they finally find Him, His mother says, 'Son, why have you treated us like this?' And Jesus replies, 'Why were you searching for me? Didn't you know I had to be in my Father's house?'

"Jesus didn't answer his mother's question, or did He? He wasn't trying to irritate her. He answered her question with two questions instead of giving her a direct answer. He had, in fact, answered her question. He phrased it in the form of a question to make her think.

"When I answer your questions with a question, I either believe you already know the answer, or I'm trying to make you think. Getting back to your question about my bookmarks, you asked me if you could shorten the title. I believe you already know the answer to that." I did know the answer. I wrote out the whole title on the next index card.

Answering a question with a question must be a pastor thing. I was having a conversation with my pastor, Jonathan Lange, when he began answering my questions with questions, as usual. I asked him his reasons for doing so, and he replied, "I don't do that, do I?" I told him that, yes, he did and casually mentioned that Jesus did, too. He said, "He did, didn't He?" I think Pastor Lange liked my comparison of him to Jesus, even if it was just in answering questions with questions, and I was pleased that I could pass on Pastor Rogahn's insight to another pastor.

GODPARENTS

I was adding the authors' names to Pastor Rogahn's bookmarks. Most of them were shorter than the titles, so it was going pretty fast. I became bored when I got to a collection and had to write the same name on several cards. Pastor Rogahn had been on the phone most of the afternoon trying to arrange a conference with other pastors. He completed his task before I finished mine.

"I'm sorry I've been on the phone all afternoon, Judi. I would have had you come on a different day if I'd known it was going to take so long to reach everyone. We didn't have much time to talk. How's everything at school? Home?"

"Karen's starting to show now. Her belly's getting big, and, guess what? Not only am I going to be an aunt again, but she said I can be the baby's godmother, too."

"That's a big job for a fifteen year old. What do you suppose a godparent does?"

"I don't know. I guess if my sister dies, I get the baby."

"I'm sure Karen's husband would have something to say about that. Did your sister tell you anything about what your role will be as the baby's godmother?"

"Yeah, she said I could hold the baby during the baptism and not to wear jeans or anything that would embarrass her. She said she felt bad because she had asked me to be the maid of honor at her wedding, but her friend Carla got mad at her, so she asked me if Carla could be the maid of honor instead. I said okay, but I guess she still feels guilty about it because she's making me a godmother, which is fine with me, because I'd rather be the baby's godmother than a goofy maid of honor."

"You've told me what your role is going to be during the baptism and why she chose you as a sponsor, but you still haven't told me what your responsibility is as a godparent. Do you know?"

"I have a feeling you're going to tell me."

"I am because I think you should know. I believe you can handle the role; you just need someone to tell you what it is. Your job is to pray for the baby and remind him or her of his baptism. And if something *would* happen to your sister, or if she should fail to do her job as a Christian parent, then you need to do it. You need to teach the child everything you learned: the Ten Commandments, the Lord's Prayer, everything that would help the child grow to lead a godly life to the honor and glory of Jesus."

"I've got to do all that? I thought I just had to hold the baby and try not to do anything goofy during the ceremony. I don't know if I can do all that."

"That's your responsibility as a godparent. It would make it easier on you, of course, if Karen performs her role as a Christian mother."

"Maybe I'll just make sure Karen performs her role as a Christian mother."

"I would call that being a good godparent."

Karen had a baby girl she named Holly Elizabeth. Pastor Rogahn performed the baptism ceremony, and, as far as I can remember, I didn't do anything to embarrass my sister.

Holly attended Messiah School through the fourth grade. My sister performed her role as a Christian mother, so my role as a godparent was easy.

BONDAGE

Pastor Rogahn was reviewing the newsletter for any last minute changes. I was adding the number of pages in each book to his bookmarks. I was lost in my own reverie, having just learned one of my friends was gay.

I had never discussed any kind of sexual issues with Pastor Rogahn before. What could a pastor know about sex? Did they even have sex? Maybe just to have kids. And what about homosexuals? I wondered if the Bible had anything to say about them. I was trying to think of a way to bring up the subject without embarrassing him or myself. But he would know. Finally I just blurted it out.

"Say, Pastor, I was just wondering if there's anything in the Bible about gays? My friend Jeremy said God created gays, too. He obviously did if he created Jeremy, right? Jeremy says he doesn't have a choice because he's not attracted to girls. He was born that way. Jeremy's a Christian, Pastor."

"Judi, homosexuality is just one of many sinful conditions in people. And whether someone believes he is born that way or not doesn't matter. Every person is in bondage to sin in some way or another; that's why Jesus came. When He died on the cross and rose again from the dead, He showed that He has the power to undo *every* kind of bondage to sin. Our job is to love each person God brings our way and tell them that when Jesus becomes the Lord of their life, He will change their hearts and deliver them completely. That goes for homosexuality, alcoholism, addiction to smoking, and even the love of gossip, just to name a few."

"But Jeremy loves God, Pastor. He's a Christian."

"Many people who call themselves Christians have not discovered some of the best news in the Bible—that when they surrender their own will to the Lord and allow Him to take over their lives, He will demonstrate His power through the Holy Spirit to do things that seemed impossible. In Galatians it says, 'It is not I who live, but Christ who lives in me.'

"When the Lord has changed our hearts like this, then the Holy Spirit enables us to obey God. In fact, He changes us into people who long to obey Him and live in a way that's pleasing to Him. Pray for Jeremy to fully surrender his life to the Lord. You can be sure the Lord is well able to do the rest. And there's more good news! Tell Jeremy that when the Lord is running his life, he'll also lose all his worry and anxiety. He'll truly know that peace Jesus promised to give us."

Jeremy was delivered from the bondage of homosexuality about ten years later. Since then, of course, I have met others who are homosexual, alcoholic, and in many other kinds of bondage. I continue to pray for them and share the good news of God's deliverance whenever I have the chance.

PEACE

I stormed into Pastor Rogahn's office, slammed my books down on the table, pulled out a chair, and slouched down in it. He was sitting at his desk, writing.

"What do you want me to do?" I asked him in a grumpy voice.

"I want you to tell me what's the matter," he said, setting his pen down and giving me his full attention. "You're obviously upset about something."

"I just hate school, that's all. There's nothing you can do about it." I folded my arms across my chest and slumped down a little more, stretching my legs out.

"Why do you hate school?" he asked. "I thought things were going well for you since you got your own column."

"That's just one class, Pastor," I said. "There's a lot more to going to high school than just writing a column. Maybe you can't remember back that far."

"Maybe I can't," he agreed. "Why don't you refresh my dusty old memory?"

"Well, I don't know how bad it was back when you went. But I've got an anthropology teacher who gives a test every Friday. My economics teacher is dumber than the dumbest kid in the class. My geometry teacher tells stupid jokes all day. It's just boring, that's all. I can't wait until I turn sixteen next year so I can quit."

"A year is a long time away, Judi," Pastor Rogahn said. "It doesn't sound like you want to wait a whole year to get a little peace. You want peace right now, don't you?"

I sat up a little straighter in my chair. Maybe he *could* help me.

"You bet I do," I replied, "but you can't quit school in the state of Missouri until you turn sixteen. It's the law, Pastor."

He stroked his chin and thought about it for a minute.

"Let me think about this," he said. "You can't quit school for a year, but how are you going to make it through your whole, boring sophomore year until you *can* quit? Oh, and I didn't think about when you do quit, you're going to miss everything you would have learned in your junior and senior years. Maybe this school year won't be so boring after all because you're going to have to cram what you would have learned during those two years into this year, so you can get a job when you do quit. But you want peace right now. You don't want more work and more stress. You just want some peace."

"That's right, Pastor," I nodded. "I just want some peace, just a little peace from that stupid, boring school."

"You can have it," he said, "but the only way to have peace is to turn everything over to Jesus, to take it one day at a time. You can't have peace when you're making plans way into next year, and you're making them by yourself. Turn everything—the stupid anthropology, the dumb economics, the boring geometry—over to Jesus, and you'll have peace because Jesus *is* peace."

"That's your solution?" I groaned. "That's not a solution at all. I still have to go back to that crummy school tomorrow, and I still hate it."

"I thought you wanted peace," he said. "You're still talking about tomorrow. Tomorrow isn't any different than next year. You don't know what's going to happen tomorrow. Put tomorrow in..."

"I do know what's going to happen tomorrow," I said, cutting him off. "I've got a test in anthropology that I didn't study for, I've got..."

"Peace," Pastor Rogahn said. "Jesus is peace, Judi. His first words when He arose from the dead were 'Peace be with you.' He knows how much we all need peace. You worry more than you need to. I'm sure you'll do fine on your test, and you'll survive the rest of the semester with the dumb teacher and the dumb jokes. Just turn everything over to Jesus, and take things one day at a time. Are you feeling *any* more peaceful than you were when you first got here?"

"I guess so," I replied. I didn't know if I felt better because I'd blown off some steam or because talking with Pastor Rogahn made me realize I couldn't change anything. But I did feel better. Maybe it wouldn't hurt to try to turn things over to Jesus and take things one day at a time. I might get a little peace and survive the semester.

"What do you want added to your bookmarks today?" I was ready to get to work. I had a little more energy than when I had first come in.

"I'm calling a book tender's holiday," he said. "I think I can live with my bookmarks the way they are for a couple more weeks. I'm giving you the afternoon off to clear your mind and to get a little peace, and you know where you can find peace. If you want to use the time to study for your test, well, that's up to you."

"Thanks, Pastor," I said as I walked peacefully out of his office.

GOOD-BYE

I have heard it said that smell is the sense which triggers memories for most people—the sweaty odor of a worn baseball glove, the stale scent of a musty old house, or the smell of a freshly mowed lawn.

For me it is sound. The popping sound of a bottle cap when a beer is opened. The clanking sound of one bottle hitting others when it's tossed into a trash can. The sound of footsteps—two forward and one back— when someone walks up the stairs drunk. . .the knocking sound a body makes when it's thrown against a wall, the brushing sound it makes when it's dragged across the floor, and the thumping sound it makes when it's kicked down the stairs. . .

The sound of Pastor Rogahn's voice.

"Hi, old friend."

I am his old friend now. It is spring 1987, and I'm twenty-five. I'm wearing a skirt and sweater. At sixteen, I stopped praying to be a boy when I realized and accepted that it wasn't God's will.

My old friend Pastor Rogahn. I've known him nearly half my life. I've come to say good-bye. He has accepted a call to Peace Lutheran Church in Mill Valley, California. I want him to stay.

"You don't need me, Judi. You need God."

"I need you more than I need God."

"God has a purpose for everything. If he wants me in California, this move will be better for everyone, including Messiah, including you."

"It just doesn't feel right."

"You'll get used to it. You're welcome to call or write to me anytime."

"But Pastor," I pleaded, as I wiped the tears from my eyes, "who's going to tend to your books?"

He embraced me in a fatherly hug.

"I do have a lot of books to pack, don't I? I'll miss you, Judi, and I love you. I love you because you're a member of Messiah and a child of God, but I also love you because you're you, because you're Judi."

I wish I had said, "I love you, too," but those words weren't part of my vocabulary then. I regret it now.

"Thanks, Pastor. I'll miss you, too."

I glanced at the bookshelves as I walked out of his office. They were arranged by colors, with all of his red books first.

Epilogue

"I've accepted the call to California. I'll be leaving in a month."

"No, Pastor. I need you to stay."

"You don't need me. You need God."

"I need you more than I need God."

Sounds. Baby Josiah is crying in the background. Tami is trying to comfort him. The other four children are laughing and talking. It is August 2003, and I'm forty-two. I'm on the phone with Pastor Jonathan Lange. He has just accepted a call to St. Paul's Lutheran Church in Merced, California.

Pastor Lange looks much younger than his thirty-six years, but he often seems more like an older brother to me. He has a delightful sense of humor and a lot of Pastor Rogahn's wisdom. His father and brother are also Lutheran pastors.

"God has a purpose for everything, Taylor. If he wants me in California, this move will be better for everyone, including Messiah, including you."

I've been Taylor for over ten years. I have tried to leave Judi and all her baggage behind.

"It just doesn't feel right."

"You'll get used to it. You can email me, and you and Rick can bring the kids for a visit. I'm going to miss seeing your children grow up. I'll miss you and Rick, too. I love you."

"I love you, too, Pastor."

My conversation with Pastor Lange triggered memories of Pastor Rogahn. I went to the computer, switched it on and began typing.

"It seems only fitting that I should be writing a book…"

The Reverend Kenneth W. Rogahn, Ph.D.

About Pastor Rogahn

Kenneth W. Rogahn was born February 16, 1933, in Milwaukee, Wisconsin. He married Su McKemie in 1958, and they have one son David.

Pastor Rogahn was ordained at Faith Lutheran Church in Milwaukee, Wisconsin, in 1960 and was called to Our Redeemer Lutheran Church in Dubuque, Iowa, where he served until 1963. He was then called to Immanuel Lutheran Church in Whitestone, New York, where he stayed until 1965, when he took a teaching position at Martin Luther High School in Maspeth, New York.

In 1968 he returned to the ministry with a call to Messiah Lutheran Church in Princeton, New Jersey. He was called to Trinity Lutheran Church in Anna, Illinois, in 1972, where he stayed until Messiah called him in 1975. His final call was to Peace Lutheran Church in Mill Valley, California in 1987.

Pastor Rogahn earned his Ph.D. from Concordia Seminary-St. Louis in 1975. He is the author of three books: *Parables From the Cross* (1982) *Glory in the Cross* (1985) *Begin With Prayer* (1985).

Pastor Rogahn died on March 16, 1991, in Mill Valley, California, four years after leaving Messiah. He was fifty-eight years old.

—To Order—

It Was Never About Books:
Conversations Between a Teen and Her Pastor
by J. Taylor Ludwig

If not available at your favorite bookstore,
you may order directly from
LangMarc Publishing
P.O. 90488
Austin, Texas 78709-0488
or call toll free
1-800-864-1648
or order online
www.langmarc.com

U.S.A.: $10.95 + $2.50 shipping
(Texas residents: add 90 cents sales tax)
Canada: $13.95 + postage
Send check or money order
Credit cards accepted

Send _____ copies of *It Was Never About Books*

To: _____

Address: _____

_____

Telephone: _____

Check enclosed: $ _____

Credit card: _____

Expiration: _____

NOTES

NOTES

Printed in the United States
35701LVS00002B/256-321